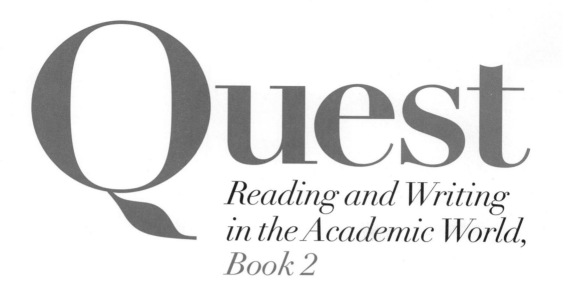

Quest

Reading and Writing in the Academic World, Book 2

Pamela Hartmann
Los Angeles Unified School District

D1408513

**McGraw-Hill
College**

Boston   Burr Ridge, IL   Dubuque, IA   Madison, WI
New York   San Francisco   St. Louis
Bangkok   Bogotá   Caracas   Lisbon   London
Madrid   Mexico City   Milan   New Delhi   Seoul
Singapore   Sydney   Taipei   Toronto

McGraw-Hill College

A Division of The **McGraw·Hill** *Companies*

QUEST: READING AND WRITING IN THE ACADEMIC WORLD, BOOK 2

This book is printed on acid-free paper.

1 2 3 4 5 6 7 8 9 0 QPF/QPF 9 3 2 1 0 9 8

ISBN 0–07–006260–9

Editorial director: *Thalia Dorwick*
Publisher: *Tim Stookesberry*
Developmental editor: *Pam Tiberia*
Marketing manager: *Tracy R. Landrum*
Project manager: *Sherry Padden*
Production supervisor: *Sandra Hahn*
Designer: *Michael Warrell*
Senior photo research coordinator: *Carrie K. Burger*
Art editor: *Joyce Watters*
Supplement coordinator: *Stacy A. Patch*
Compositor: *David Corona Design*
Typeface: *10/12 Times Roman*
Printer: *Quebecor Printing Book Group/Fairfield, PA*

Cover designer: *Victory Productions*
Cover image: *Lonnie Sue Johnson*
Art done by: *Electra Graphics*

www.mhhe.com

contents

unit 1
Global Business   1

chapter one
Doing Business Internationally   3

chapter two
International Economy 37

unit 2
Art   69

chapter three
Themes and Purposes   71

chapter four
The Ancient World: Egypt   107

preface

Quest: The Series

The *Quest* series addresses the need to prepare students for the demands of college-level academic coursework. *Quest* differs from other content-based ESOL series in that it incorporates material typically covered in general education courses, and contains a variety of academic areas including biology, business, U.S. history, psychology, art history, cultural anthropology, American literature, and economics.

 Quest has been designed to parallel and accelerate the process that native speakers of English go through when they study core required subjects in high school. By previewing typical college course material, *Quest* helps students get "up to speed" in terms of both academic content and language skills.

 In addition, *Quest* prepares students for the daunting amount and level of reading, writing, listening, and speaking required for college success. The three *Reading and Writing* books combine high-interest material from newspapers and magazines with traditional academic source materials such as textbooks. Reading passages increase in length and difficulty across the three levels. The *Listening and Speaking* books in the *Quest* series contain listening strategies and practice activities based on authentic recordings from "person on the street" interviews, radio programs, and college lectures. Similar to the *Reading and Writing* books, the three *Listening and Speaking* books increase in difficulty with each level.

Quest: Reading and Writing in the Academic World, Book 2

Quest: Reading and Writing in the Academic World, Book 2 is designed for students at an intermediate to high-intermediate level of proficiency, and contains many unique features that were introduced in *Book 1,* including the use of a word journal and self- and peer editing checklists. Four distinct units each focus on a different area of college study—Global Business, Art, Psychology, and Health. Each content unit contains two chapters. The Global Business unit contains chapters on doing business internationally and international economy, and the Art unit includes chapters on themes and purposes and the ancient world (Egypt). The third unit is on Psychology and features chapters concentrating on states of consciousness and abnormal psychology. The last unit, Health, contains a chapter on medicine and drugs (addictive substances) and a chapter on the secrets of good health.

Unique Chapter Structure

Each chapter of *Quest: Reading and Writing in the Academic World, Book 2* contains five parts that blend reading and writing skills within the context of a particular academic area of study. Readings and activities build upon one another and increase in difficulty as students work through the five sections of each chapter. Parts One and Two include reading selections that introduce the chapter topic and revolve around cutting-edge ideas, events, people in the news, and cross-cultural issues. These first two parts of each chapter prepare students for the academic material that appears in Part Three, where students read an authentic textbook passage and work on academic reading skills such as recognizing general and specific ideas, finding important details, and synthesizing ideas.

After students have gained exposure to the content area and have practiced reading skills and strategies in Parts One through Three, they move on to developing clear and effective writing skills. Part Four introduces basic writing mechanics and includes content-based grammar topics. In Part Five, students focus on writing process skills as they complete a culminating writing assignment that incorporates both the content area knowledge and the writing skills that they have practiced and developed earlier in the chapter. For a complete list of the reading and writing skills found in this book, consult the Reading and Writing Skills Chart on pages xi–xii.

Instructor's Manual*

The Instructor's Manual to accompany *Quest: Reading and Writing in the Academic World, Books 1–3* provides instructors with a general outline of the series, as well as detailed teaching suggestions and important information regarding levels and placement, classroom management, and chapter organization. For each of the three books, there is a separate section with answer keys, optional editing exercises, and unit tests.

Acknowledgments

Many, many thanks go to those who made this series possible: publisher for ESOL, Tim Stookesberry, who first said *yes;* editorial director Thalia Dorwick, who made it happen; editors Bill Preston and Pam Tiberia, who gave encouragement and support and helped shape the manuscript; photo researcher Toni Michaels, who truly understands the relationship between text and image (and who actually got us the opossums); project manager Sherry Padden, designer Michael Warrell, and the entire production team; and the following reviewers, whose opinions were invaluable: Betty Wheeler, Pamela McPartland-Fairman, Glenn Hawes, John Dumicich, Christine Root, Thomas Adams, Bernadette Garcia, Gail Barta, Helen Huntley, Jackie Stembridge, Robin Longshaw, and Colleen Revillini.

---

* The supplement listed here accompanies *Quest: Reading and Writing in the Academic World, Books 1–3.* Please contact your local McGraw-Hill representative for details concerning policies, prices, and availability as some restrictions may apply.

visual tour
Highlights of this Book

Visually Captivating Photo and Art Program

Part One of each chapter in *Quest* typically begins with a discussion of a photo that introduces the chapter topic. In this example, students examine an Egyptian wall painting and answer questions that serve as a springboard for the first reading. (page 108)

Unit 2 Art

⁚⁚⁚⁞⁞ Part One Rules of Egyptian Art

Before Reading

Discussion. Look at the following wall painting. In small groups, examine the details of the painting and answer these questions.

1. Which people are Nakht and his wife? Why do you think so?
2. Who might the other people be?
3. What are the people doing? Describe as many activities as possible.
4. Do these figures look realistic? Why or why not? What seems strange about them?

Nakht and His Wife. Copy of a wall painting from the tomb of Nakht, c. 1425 BC, Thebes, Egypt. The Metropolitan Museum of Art, New York.

Chapter Four The Ancient World: Egypt 109

Reading

As you read the following passage, think about the answer to this question

* Why did the style of Egyptian art stay almost the same for 3,000 years?

The Rules of Egyptian Art

Just for a few moments, imagine some famous paintings of one or two hundred years ago. Can you picture these in your mind? Now imagine the most modern abstract art of today. In only one to two hundred years, there have been huge changes in the form and content of art. In contrast, the characteristics of ancient Egyptian art remained nearly the same for almost three thousand ye
Man
tian art
famous
which w

Rules for Artists

1. The pharaoh (king) or most important person must be the largest. Servants, children, and unimportant wives must be smaller.
2. Men have dark or red skin. Women have light or yellow skin. (It doesn't matter what their real skin color is.)
3. People of high status—especially the pharaoh—must look stiff and serious. They should appear frozen and unmoving.
4. People of low status may be shown in more natural positions as they hunt, fish, plant or harvest crops, and do other work.
5. Depict animals as naturally as possible in correct biological details.

High-Interest Readings

This reading on the rules of Egyptian art captures students' attention and motivates them to find out even more about the chapter topic. (pages 109–110).

Emphasis on Reading Preparation

All readings are preceded by pre-reading activities such as prediction and vocabulary preparation. In activity B, students make guesses about words that they will encounter in the reading entitled "Finds Reveal Much of Life at Pyramids." (page 112)

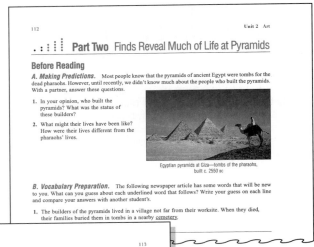

Reading Strategy Boxes

Reading Strategy boxes occur throughout each chapter and provide students with practical skills they can use immediately as they begin each new reading passage. In this example, students are given guidance in how to guess meaning from context. (page 113)

Reading Selections Build in Length and Complexity

The reading selections in each chapter of *Quest* increase in length and complexity and finish with an authentic textbook passage that appears in Part Three. Authentic readings are supported with practice in a variety of academic reading skills such as recognizing tone, identifying causes and effects, and making inferences. (pages 119, 124)

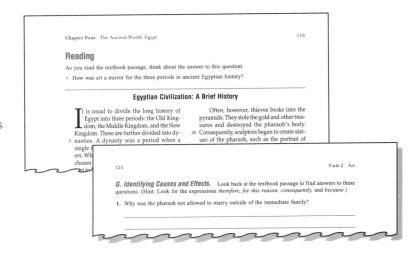

Abundance of Practice Material

Each of the readings is followed by a wide variety of exercises that help to solidify students' comprehension of new material and vocabulary. In activity E, students are asked to log new vocabulary in a word journal. Students are encouraged to use a word journal to keep track of new words and definitions that they learn throughout the course. (page 123)

Chapter Four   The Ancient World: Egypt   123

D. Vocabulary Expansion.   Your vocabulary will grow faster if you learn different parts of speech when you learn a new word. Use the textbook passage and a dictionary to fill in these words.

Verb		Noun	
_____		succession	(situation)
		successor	(person)
_____		_____	(situation)
		ruler	(person)
establish		_____	
restore		_____	

E. Word Journal.   Go back to the passage. Which words are important for you to remember? Put them in your Word Journal.

Part Four   The Mechanics of Writing

In Part Five, you are going to write a paragraph about Egyptian art. In your paragraph, you'll need to explain the artist's reasons for the style of a painting. Part Four will help you to write about causes, effects, and purposes.

Infinitives of Purpose

An infinitive (*to* + the simple form of a verb) can answer the question "Why."

Example: Artists depicted the pharaoh as stiff and unmoving <u>to show</u> his high status.

   (<u>to show</u> his high status = because they wanted to show his high status)

Solid Introduction to the Mechanics of Writing

Part Four is devoted to providing students with chapter-specific writing mechanics that better equip them to express their ideas in the writing assignment that follows in Part Five. Only necessary techniques and skills that will be used in Part Five are included in the mechanics section. (page 124)

Content-Driven Grammar Boxes

Grammatical, lexical, and punctuation information is clearly presented in an easy-to-read boxed format. These boxes are followed by contextualized practice activities that prepare students for their independent writing assignment at the end of the chapter. In this example, students practice using transitional expressions and phrases in a paragraph about pyramids. (page 127)

Chapter Four   The Ancient World: Egypt   127

Transitional Expressions and Phrases

If the cause or reason is a noun or noun phrase (instead of a clause), use <u>due to</u> or <u>because of</u>.

Examples: Skilled artisans were buried in tombs of better quality <u>because of</u> their higher status.
   (noun phrase)

   <u>Because of</u> their higher status, skilled artisans were buried in tombs of better quality.
   (noun phrase)

C. Practice.   In the following paragraph, fill in the blanks with <u>because</u>, <u>since</u>, <u>as</u>, <u>because of</u>, or <u>due to</u>. Don't use the same expression more than once.

_____ ancient Egyptian religious beliefs, much of what we know today about the people comes from their tombs. Great care was taken to protect and preserve the body after death _____ people believed that a person's *ka*, or soul, needed a body in which to live. It was especially necessary to preserve the body of the pharaoh _____ he was seen as both a king and a god. People believed that he would join the other gods when he died. _____

Chapter-Culminating Focus on Writing

Each chapter culminates in a writing assignment found in Part Five. This assignment is based on the chapter readings and themes and incorporates the writing mechanics that students practiced in the previous section. In each chapter, students are led through the writing process, which at different times may include brainstorming, narrowing the topic, writing topic sentences, planning the writing, and developing ideas into a paragraph. (page 129)

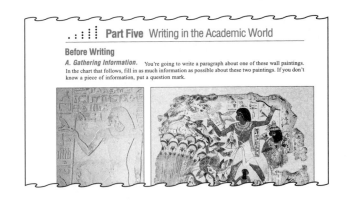

Carefully Directed Writing Assignments

Writing assignments focus on a variety of rhetorical styles. This chart helps students prepare to write a paragraph about causes, effects, and purposes. Assignments in other chapters include paragraphs of persuasion, definition, example, and analysis. (page 130)

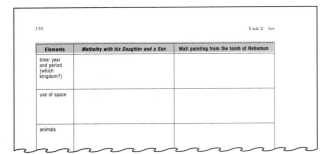

Writing Strategy Boxes

Writing Strategy boxes offer students various writing tips and suggestions. In this example, students learn how to write a paragraph of cause and effect such as those typically necessary in essay tests. (page 131)

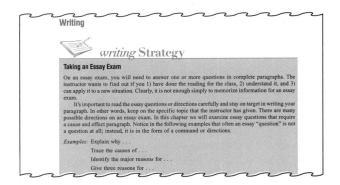

Self- and Peer Editing

A self- and peer editing checklist concludes each writing assignment and guides students toward the kinds of changes they will need to make in the second draft of their writing. (page 133)

summary of Reading and Writing Skills

Chapter	Reading Skills	Mechanics and Writing Skills
1	• making inferences • dealing with new words • guessing meaning from context: using definitions or synonyms after a comma, dash, or in parentheses • skimming for main topics • finding the main idea • finding details • understanding stems and affixes	• simple present and simple past tenses • modals of advice (present, future, past) • the subject *you* (meaning "everyone") • adjective clauses (relative clauses) • coordinating conjunctions • introduction to brainstorming, choosing a topic, narrowing a topic, planning a paragraph • paragraph of example
2	• understanding new words: accepting uncertainty • making inferences • understanding parts of speech • introduction to the use of a word journal • understanding italics • guessing meaning from context: information in the next sentence; the phrases *that is* and *in other words* • marking a book	• the passive voice • adverbial conjunctions • avoiding and repairing run-ons and comma splices • writing a topic sentence • gathering information • organizing supporting material • paragraph of analysis
3	• determining point of view • thinking ahead • understanding subject and object pronouns • finding similarities and differences • understanding italics	• appositives • adjective clauses • participial phrases • prepositional phrases • adjectives: basic rules • order of adjectives • transitional expressions of comparison-contrast • identifying a good topic sentence • gathering and organizing supporting material • paragraph of comparison-contrast

Chapter	Reading Skills	Mechanics and Writing Skills
4	• making predictions • guessing meaning from context: using opposites • understanding idioms • recognizing tone • identifying causes and effects • making inferences • understanding stems and affixes	• infinitives of purpose • subordinating conjunctions of cause and effect • transitional expressions and phrases • conjunctions of cause and effect: review • taking an essay exam • paragraph of description/ cause and effect
5	• determining point of view • identifying general and specific ideas • choosing the correct dictionary definition • synthesizing information	• transition words of time (subordinating and adverbial conjunctions) • use of tenses in narration • writing about symbols • idea mapping • using variety in language • paragraph of narration • paragraph of analysis
6	• finding important details • making inferences • understanding stems and affixes	• the passive voice • adjective clauses in definitions: review • writing about advantages and disadvantages • adverbial conjunctions of addition and contradiction • paraphrasing • summarizing • citing sources • paragraph of summary (including advantages and disadvantages)
7	• understanding metaphors • pronoun reference	• subordinating conjunctions: review/extension • avoiding and repairing fragments • the present unreal conditional • writing a topic sentence for a persuasive paragraph • paragraph of persuasion
8	• making inferences • understanding possessive adjectives	• using italics and quotation marks (summary) • review of conjunctions of contradiction and cause and effect • writing definitions • paragraph of definition

CURRENCY CROSSRATES					
	Dollar	Pound	SF	Peseta	DFL
Belgium	32.517	49.914	24.495	.24836	18.388
Canada	1.3695	2.1021	1.0316	.01046	.77440
ECU	.82645	1.2686	.62256	.00631	.46734
France	5.4030	8.2936	4.0701	.04127	3.0553
Germany	1.5755	2.4184	1.1868	.01203	
Italy	1584.0	2431.4	1183.2	12.099	895.72
Japan	99.51	152.76	74.957	.7600	54.288
Netherlands	1.7684	2.7145	1.3321	.01354	
Spain	130.83	200.87	98.622		
Switzerland	1.3276	2.0377		74.439	1.9
U.K.	.65100		.01343		
U.S.		1.5360	.7539	.00774	

EUROCURRENCY

Global Business

chapter One

Doing Business Internationally

In this chapter, you'll read and write about the importance of understanding culture in doing global business.

. .:::: **Part One** International Advertising

Before Reading

Discussion.   Look at the various magazine advertisements (ads) on pages 4 and 5. Answer these questions with a partner.

1. From which countries do these products come?

2. What languages do you see? In which countries are the companies selling these products?

3. Which of these products do you have in your country?

a.

b.

c.

d.

Reading

Read these two paragraphs. Think about the answer to this question.

* What mistake did these two companies make?

International Advertising

One laundry detergent company certainly now realizes its mistake. It probably wishes that it had asked for the opinion of some Arabic speakers before it started its new advertising program in the Middle East. All of the company's advertisements showed dirty clothes on the left, its box of soap in the middle, and clean clothes on the right. But people read Arabic from right to left, not left to right. For this reason, many potential customers saw the ad and thought, "This soap makes clothes dirty!"

Source: "International Advertising" (editor's title, originally titled, and adapted from, "Elements of Culture"), from Alan M. Rugman and Richard M. Hodgetts, *International Business: A Strategic Management Approach, International Edition*, page 126, Copyright © 1995 by McGraw-Hill, Inc. Reprinted with the permission of the publishers.

15 An anthropologist with many years of experience in Brazil, Conrad Phillip Kottak noted the advertising for McDonald's when the fast-food restaurant first opened in Rio de Janeiro. *20* The advertisements listed several "favorite places where you can enjoy McDonald's products." Clearly, the marketing people were trying to fit their product into Brazilian middle- *25* class culture, but they made some mistakes. One suggestion was to visit McDonald's "when you go out in the car with the kids." It seems that the writer of this ad never tried to drive *30* up to a fast-food restaurant in a neighborhood with no parking places. Also not very helpful was the suggestion to eat McDonald's hamburgers "at a picnic at the beach." This ignored the *35* Brazilian custom of consuming cold things, such as beer, soft drinks, ice cream, and ham and cheese sandwiches, at a beach picnic. It's hard enough to keep sand off an ice cream *40* cone. Brazilians do not consider a hot, greasy hamburger proper beach food.

Source: "International Advertising" (editor's title, originally titled, and adapted from, "Culture and International Marketing"), from Conrad Phillip Kottak, *Anthropology: The Exploration of Human Diversity, Fifth Edition,* page 399. Copyright © 1991, 1987, 1982, 1978, 1974 by McGraw-Hill, Inc. Reprinted with the permission of the publishers.

After Reading

A. Main Ideas.   With a partner, answer these questions.

1. What was the mistake in the laundry detergent advertisement?
2. What were two mistakes in the McDonald's advertisement?

 reading Strategy

Making Inferences

Sometimes writers don't state (say) something directly. Readers have to infer (guess or figure out) the meaning.

Example: You read: The company certainly now realizes its mistake. It probably wishes that it had asked for the opinion of some Arabic speakers.

You infer: The company didn't ask for the opinion of Arabic speakers.

Example: You read: One suggestion was to visit McDonald's "when you go out in the car with the kids." It seems that the writer of this ad never tried to drive up to a fast-food restaurant in a neighborhood with no parking places.

You infer: The neighborhood around the McDonald's in Rio didn't have parking places.

B. Making Inferences.   Infer the answer to this question: Why did McDonald's make these cultural mistakes in its advertising? Write your answer on a piece of paper. Then compare your answer with other students'.

C. Response Writing.   Choose *one* of these topics:

* a popular product in your country that comes from another country

* a popular foreign company or business in your country that has changed something about the lifestyle (the way people live) in your culture

* a popular product or company in the United States or Canada that comes from your country

    In a separate notebook or a separate section in your three-ring binder, write about your topic for ten minutes. Don't worry about grammar and don't stop writing to use a dictionary. You don't need to worry about being "correct." You won't give this paper to your teacher. Just put as many ideas as possible on paper.

. : : : : : **Part Two** How Is Your Cross-Cultural Business IQ?

Before Reading

A. Discussion.   Look at the pictures on pages 7 and 8. Answer these questions with a partner.

1. Where are the people in each picture? What are they doing?

2. Can you think of some possible problems for people who do business in different countries?

3. Before you travel to another country, what information do you need to have about the culture (way of life) in that country?

a.

b.

c.

d.

B. Understanding New Words.   When you're learning a new language, you always find many new words. You will save time and enjoy the language more if you *guess* the meaning of many new words—form an opinion about them without a dictionary. Practice with the advertisements below. In your opinion, what is the question on the left? What is the answer on the right? What is the company advertising? (A dictionary won't help you with these words!)

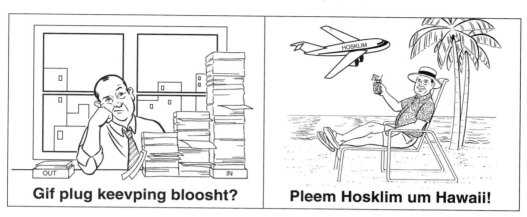

Gif plug keevping bloosht?   **Pleem Hosklim um Hawaii!**

reading **Strategy**

What to Do When You Find a New Word

You will always find new words when you read textbooks in English. It's important *not* to use a dictionary for every new word. Instead, follow these steps.

Step 1. Try to guess the meaning of a new word from the context. The context is the sentence or paragraph that the word is in.

Step 2. If you can guess the meaning, don't use a dictionary (even if you don't understand the *exact* meaning).

Step 3. Sometimes the context is too limited (short, not helpful), or there are too many new words, so you can't guess the meaning. What should you do? Decide how important the word is.

Step 4. If the word isn't essential (absolutely necessary), don't worry about it. Just keep reading.

Step 5. If the word is essential and you can't understand the sentence or paragraph without it, you'll need to use a monolingual (English-English) dictionary. Your teacher can suggest one.

C. Practice.   Use the steps from the box. If it is possible to guess *anything* about the word, write your guess on the line. Don't use a dictionary. (Note: These are just nonsense words—not real words.) Follow the examples.

1. It's especially important to <u>mebegle</u>.

Is it possible to guess the meaning?   Yes   (No)   Yes, but not exactly

If yes, my guess: _____

If no, is the word important?   (Yes)   No

2. This is one of the largest <u>ebbists</u> (companies) in the country.

Is it possible to guess the meaning?   (Yes)   No   Yes, but not exactly

If yes, my guess: _____*companies*_____

If no, is the word important?   Yes   No

3. He picked up the <u>lazzapilt</u> and began to read.

Is it possible to guess the meaning?   Yes   No   Yes, but not exactly

If yes, my guess: _____

If no, is the word important?   Yes   No

4. The music was playing so <u>tubbly</u> that it hurt my ears.

Is it possible to guess the meaning?   Yes   No   Yes, but not exactly

If yes, my guess: _____

If no, is the word important?   Yes   No

5. We caught three <u>sibglits</u> and some other fish, too.

Is it possible to guess the meaning?   Yes   No   Yes, but not exactly

If yes, my guess: _____

If no, is the word important?   Yes   No

6. She stood up and <u>mished</u> out of the room.

Is it possible to guess the meaning? Yes No Yes, but not exactly

If yes, my guess: _____

If no, is the word important? Yes No

7. I often <u>lubtrizzled</u> when I was a child.

Is it possible to guess the meaning? Yes No Yes, but not exactly

If yes, my guess: _____

If no, is the word important? Yes No

8. The two little boys always played together. They were <u>umithers</u>.

Is it possible to guess the meaning? Yes No Yes, but not exactly

If yes, my guess: _____

If no, is the word important? Yes No

9. A big, wet, <u>skapit</u> dog shook water all over us.

Is it possible to guess the meaning? Yes No Yes, but not exactly

If yes, my guess: _____

If no, is the word important? Yes No

10. They studied several <u>purlams</u>—Buddhism, Judaism, Christianity, and Islam.

Is it possible to guess the meaning? Yes No Yes, but not exactly

If yes, my guess: _____

If no, is the word important? Yes No

Reading

Take this test just for fun. Don't worry about "right" or "wrong" answers. If you know an answer, circle its letter. If you don't know an answer, put a question mark. You'll find out the correct answers later. Don't use a dictionary. Try to guess new words. You'll practice vocabulary after the test.

How Is Your Cross-Cultural Business IQ?

1. In Arab countries, when a man greets another man who has higher status—social position—he should

   a. immediately shake hands.

   b. wait until the other man offers to shake hands.

   c. not shake hands because it's impolite to touch a person he doesn't know.

2. In Turkey, you shouldn't

   a. shake hands.

   b. stand up when an older person enters the room.

   c. sit with crossed legs.

3. In the United States, when a man greets an American businesswoman, he should

   a. shake hands gently because she is a woman.

   b. shake hands firmly and have eye contact.

   c. not shake hands.

4. Two Latin American businessmen are discussing a mutual acquaintance (a person whom they both know). One of the men hits his arm at the elbow. This body language means that

   a. their acquaintance is a skinflint—a miser who won't spend money.

   b. the man's elbow hurts.

   c. their acquaintance is a tennis player, a golfer, or a baseball player.

5. In Japan, when a person gives you his/her business card, you should

    a. put it in your pocket immediately.

    b. accept it with both hands, look at it, say something about it, and keep it on the table in front of you during the conversation.

    c. accept it with your right hand only and put it in your briefcase.

6. In Greece, it's important for a manager to

    a. dress very well in expensive clothes to show the employees that this person is the boss.

    b. give each employee many compliments such as "You're doing a very good job" or "That's a nice shirt."

    c. spend time with employees and learn about their families, their problems, and their lives in general.

7. If a person wants to be successful in business in Russia, it's probably not a good idea to

    a. take a business acquaintance to dinner.

    b. make some helpful suggestions about people's fashion or style of clothing.

    c. accept offers to drink vodka.

8. When you go to someone's home for dinner in Italy, France, or Russia, never bring

    a. an odd number (1, 3, 5, 7) of flowers.

    b. an even number (2, 4, 6, 8) of flowers.

    c. pink flowers.

9. When you discuss business with someone in China, be sure to

    a. use *Mr., Mrs.,* or *Ms.,* and the person's last name.

    b. use the person's first name.

    c. use the person's title such as *Chairman, President,* or *Manager.*

10. Two weeks ago, an American acquaintance said: "Let's have lunch or something sometime soon. I'll call you." But he hasn't called. Why not?

    a. He is impolite.

    b. Nothing is strange.

    c. He has a serious problem.

After Reading

reading Strategy

Guessing Meaning from Context

Sometimes it's easy to guess the meaning of a new word from the context because there's a definition or synonym after a comma (,) or dash (—) or in parentheses.

Examples: This company does business <u>globally</u> (internationally).

It's a highly successful <u>enterprise</u>—business—in our country.

In these examples, it's clear that <u>globally</u> = internationally and that <u>enterprise</u> = business.

A picture can also help you to guess the meaning of a new word.

Example: The man is hitting his <u>elbow</u>.

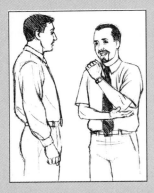

Here we see that the <u>elbow</u> = part of the arm.

Sometimes examples after the phrases *such as, for example,* or *and other* help you to know something (but maybe not everything) about a new word.

Example: We went <u>abroad</u> to places such as India, New Zealand, and Madagascar.

Here we see from the examples (India, New Zealand, and Madagascar) that <u>abroad</u> probably means "out of the country."

Often, your own experience helps you with a new word.

Example: The Brazilian custom is to <u>consume</u> cold things such as beer, soft drinks, ice cream, and ham and cheese sandwiches at a beach picnic.

Your own life experience tells you that <u>consume</u> probably means "eat and drink."

A. Practice.

What do you know about each underlined word from the context? Don't use a dictionary. Write your guess on the line.

1. He greeted the other man who had higher status—social position.

   status = _____

2. Two Latin American businessmen are discussing a mutual acquaintance (a person whom they both know).

   mutual acquaintance = _____

3. She gave many compliments such as "You're doing a very good job" or "That's a nice shirt."

   compliments = _____

4. Use the person's title such as *Chairman, President,* or *Manager.*

   title = _____

5. They brought an odd number (1, 3, 5, 7) of flowers.

   odd number = _____

6. They brought an even number (2, 4, 6, 8) of flowers.

   even number = _____

B. Practice.

Look at the test "How Is Your Cross-Cultural Business IQ?" Find other words that were new to you and write them on a piece of paper. Can you guess the meaning—or something about the meaning? If so, write your guess. If not, check with a dictionary (for essential words only). Compare your answers with another student's.

C. Discussion.

In small groups, compare your answers to the test "How Is Your Cross-Cultural Business IQ?" After you discuss all ten questions, turn to page 35 for the answers.

D. Extension.

In small groups, discuss these customs in your country.

1. What are the customs for meeting and greeting people?

2. Do you use people's names or titles—or both?

3. What are some gestures (body language) and their meaning?

4. What's a proper gift to bring if you go to someone's home?

5. What's one very important custom for businesspeople to know about?

..::::: **Part Three** Reading in the Academic World

Before Reading

A. Vocabulary Preparation.
The reading passage has some new words. You don't need a dictionary for many of them because there is a definition or synonym in the context. For each underlined word below, circle the meaning. Don't use a dictionary.

1. It's important to avoid business decisions that are based on <u>misconceptions</u>—mistaken ideas.

2. One cause of misconceptions is <u>ethnocentrism</u>—the belief that one's own culture's way of doing things is better than the way of other cultures.

3. An understanding of the language allows the person to notice the <u>implied</u> meanings and other information that is not said directly.

4. <u>Values</u> are people's basic beliefs about the difference between right and wrong, good and bad, important and unimportant.

5. An <u>attitude</u> is a way of thinking or acting.

6. <u>Manners</u> are ways of acting that the society believes are polite.

B. Thinking Ahead: Making Inferences.
Briefly discuss this cartoon with a partner. In your opinion, what is the implied meaning in the cartoon? (In other words, what does the artist mean?)

Hagar the Horrible

reading Strategy

Skimming for Main Topics

A *topic* is the subject of a paragraph or a reading passage. Textbooks often highlight topics in **bold** print. This helps students to skim a chapter—to find the main points quickly. It's possible to preview a reading for the main topics in just a few seconds.

C. Previewing.   Before you read, look over very quickly the textbook passage "International Culture." What are the five topics? Write them here.

1. _____   4. _____

2. _____   5. _____

3. _____

Reading

Read through this passage without a dictionary. Guess the meaning of each new word, if possible. Afterwards, you will practice vocabulary. As you read the passage, think about the answer to this question.

- What is necessary for success in international business?

International Culture

If people want to be successful in multinational business, they must understand the cultures of other countries and learn how to adapt to them. It's important for them to avoid business decisions that are based on misconceptions—mistaken ideas.

5   One cause of misconceptions is ethnocentrism, the belief that one's own culture's way of doing things is better than the way of other cultures. Ethnocentrism can exist in an individual person or in an organization. In the case of an individual, it takes the form of "we're better than anyone else." There are several examples of ethnocentrism in an MNE (multinational enterprise, or

10 company):

1. The company uses the same methods abroad that it uses in the home country.

2. It doesn't adapt (change) a product to fit the needs of another country.

3. It sends managers with no international experience to work abroad.

15 To avoid ethnocentrism, it's necessary to study the elements of culture. These include language, religion, values, customs, and material elements.

Language

A knowledge of the local language can help an international businessperson in four ways. First, the person can communicate directly, without someone else to translate or explain. Second, people are usually more open in their commu-
20 nication with someone who speaks their language. Third, an understanding of the language allows the person to notice the implied meanings and other information that is not said directly. Finally, language helps the person to understand the culture better.

Religion

Religion influences everything about people, including their work habits. In
25 the United States, people talk about the *Protestant work ethic*, which simply means a belief that people should work hard and save their money. In many Asian countries, the same idea is called the *Confucian work ethic*. In Japan, it is the *Shinto work ethic*.

Values and Attitudes

Values are people's basic beliefs about the
30 difference between right and wrong, good and bad, important and unimportant. An attitude is a way of thinking or acting. Values and attitudes influence international business. For example, many Russians be-
35 lieve that McDonald's food is good (value), so they wait in long lines to eat it (attitude). U.S. customers believe that chocolate from Switzerland is especially good (value), and they buy a lot of it (attitude).

> **Common Idioms That Express U.S. Business Values:**
> Time is money.
> Let's get down to business. =
> Let's get down to brass tacks.
> (= Let's begin to talk about the essential topics.)
> When in Rome, do as the Romans do.

Customs and Manners

40 Customs are common social practices. Manners are ways of acting that the society believes are polite. For example, in the United States, it is the *custom* to have salad before the main course at dinner, not after. American table *manners*

include not talking with food in the mouth and keeping the napkin in the lap, not on the table. In some countries, it is polite to arrive at a party very late, but
45 in others it is important to be on time. International businesses need to understand the customs and manners of other countries, or they will probably have difficulty selling their products. For example, an American orange juice company in France will have a problem if it sells orange juice as a breakfast drink because the French don't drink juice with breakfast.

Material Culture

50 *Material culture* means the things that people make or own. When we study material culture, we need to think about 1) how people make things (technology) and 2) who makes them and why (economics). International businesses need to consider the country's *economic infrastructure* such as transportation, communications, and energy; the *social infrastructure*—for example, the health
55 and education systems; and the *financial infrastructure,* such as banking services.

These—and other—elements of culture help to explain the differences among people of different cultures. Without an understanding of cultures, multinational enterprises cannot be successful.

Source: "International Culture" (editor's title, originally titled, and adapted from, "Elements of Culture") from Alan M. Rugman and Richard M. Hodgetts, *International Business: A Strategic Management Approach, International Edition,* pp. 124–131. Copyright © 1995 by McGraw-Hill, Inc. Reprinted with the permission of the publishers.

After Reading

reading Strategy

Finding the Main Idea

A composition or reading passage has an introduction—usually the first paragraph—and a conclusion—the last paragraph. Often, one sentence in the introduction gives the *main idea* of the reading passage. This is the most important idea. It includes all of the smaller, more specific ideas of the passage. Frequently, the main idea appears again in the conclusion, in different words.

A. Main Idea.   Look back at the passage "International Culture." Find one sentence in the first paragraph and another sentence in the last paragraph that give the main idea.

B. Vocabulary Check.
Find a word or expression in the passage for each definition. The numbers in parentheses refer to lines in the passage.

1. to change in order to fit a new situation (10–15): _____

2. the idea (in the United States) that people should
   work hard and save their money (20–25): _____

3. the things that people make or own (45–50): _____

4. how people make things (50–55): _____

5. who makes things and why (50–55): _____

6. a country's system of transportation,
   communication, and energy (50–55): _____

7. a country's health and education system (50–55): _____

8. a country's banks (50–55): _____

reading Strategy

Finding Details

Sometimes you can find important details (specific points) quickly if you look for numbers or words such as *first, second, next, finally,* etc.

C. Details.
Look back at the passage to find the answers to these questions. When you find the answers, highlight them with a felt-tip marking pen.

1. What are three examples of ethnocentrism in a multinational enterprise?

2. In what four ways can a knowledge of language help an international businessperson?

3. What two things do we need to think about when we study material culture?

 *reading* Strategy

Stems and Affixes

Parts of words, usually from Greek or Latin, will help you to guess the meaning of many new words. These word parts are *prefixes* (at the beginning of a word), *stems* (the main part of a word), and *suffixes* (the ending of a word).* Here are some examples from this passage.

Prefixes	Meaning	Stems	Meaning	Suffix	Meaning
infra-	under or within	centr	center, middle	-ism	belief in
inter-	between	ethic	moral system		
mis-	wrong	ethnic	race, culture, people		
		multi	many		

Example: m u l t i e t h n i c
              ↓   ↓
            = many   = race, culture, people

A <u>multiethnic</u> society has many different cultures.

* Prefixes and suffixes = affixes.

D. Stems and Affixes.   What do you know about these words? Use stems and affixes in the box to analyze the word parts. Work with a partner.

1. misconception   2. international   3. ethnocentrism
4. Buddhism   5. multinational

E. Application: The Elements of Culture.   For each element of culture on the following chart, write *notes*— not complete sentences—about your country. You see that some notes about American culture are on the chart as examples. Write *your opinion.* (Other people from your culture might have different answers.) You'll probably find some elements easier to write about than others. If you aren't sure about one or two elements, put a question mark and spend more time on the others. You should try your best on this exercise, however, because your writing topic in Part Five will come from this chart.

Elements of Culture	United States	(my country)
Language	mostly English; 14% non-English speakers; after English, most common langs.: Spanish, French, German, Italian, Chinese	
Religion	no state religion; many, many religs. are practiced, esp. Christianity, Judaism, Islam/many people—no relig./"Protestant work ethic"	
Values	individualism, freedom of expression (speech, writing)/"American dream"/ gender (male-female) equality/ diversity (belief in the importance of difference)/time (very valuable)	
Material Culture	private ownership of property (house, land, car, etc.) important/ but many people in debt	
Customs	a few examples: 1) Work: teenagers—part-time job in high school or college; 2) Greetings: firm handshake; 3) Strangers: "small talk" common with strangers in public places	

F. Discussion.   When you finish the chart, tell other students a little about the language, religion, values, material culture, and customs of your country and find out about their countries. Work in small groups (3–4 students).

.:::::: **Part Four** The Mechanics of Writing

In Part Five, you are going to write about your own culture. You may need to use modals of advice, adjective clauses, and the present and past tenses. You may also want to join two sentences with coordinating conjunctions. Part Four will help you to use these grammatical elements.

Tenses: Simple Present and Simple Past

The simple present tense* expresses an action that happens repeatedly (sometimes, often, frequently, every day, seldom, etc.)

Example: The British usually <u>have</u> tea in the afternoon.

The simple past tense** expresses a finished action. It is used for both short and long actions. Regular verbs end in *-ed.*

Examples: He <u>picked</u> up his knife and fork.

She <u>lived</u> in Scotland for over twenty years.

* For spelling rules for the third person, singular (*-s*), see page 245. For spelling rules for words ending in *-ed,* see page 246.

** For a list of irregular verbs, see page 247.

A. Practice. Fill in the blanks with the simple present or simple past tense of the verb in parentheses.

Equality in the Workplace

A man from another country who _____*does*_____ (do) business in North America
  1

_____ (need) to remember that in the United States, women _____
  2   3

(have) equality in the workplace. This _____ (mean) that women _____
                                                                4   5

(receive) the same pay, opportunities, and respect as men do. Sometimes this _____
                                                                                                                                  6

(be) a problem for businessmen from countries where women _____ (not have)
                                                                                                              7

positions of authority (power) in a company.

Several years ago, a multinational company _____ (open) a factory in the United
                                                          8
States. The managers _____ (be not) American. They _____
                                9   10
(be) very polite, but unfortunately, they _____ (follow) the customs for politeness
                                                      11
from their own country. For example, they _____ (treat) the women employees as
                                                      12
"helpers" with lower status than the men. These employees _____ (not appreciate)
                                                                            13
this and _____ (complain) to the upper management. The upper management
              14
_____ (not understand) the problem and _____ (not do)
              15   16
anything about it. Finally, the women _____ (feel) so frustrated that they
                                                      17
_____ (take) the company to court, where they _____ (win)
              18   19
their lawsuit.

Modals of Advice

To give advice for the present or future, use this structure:

> should
> (or)   } + the simple form of the verb
> ought to

For the negative, use *shouldn't* + the simple form of the verb.

Examples: Before you travel to another country, you <u>should learn</u> something about the culture.

A company that does business internationally <u>ought to have</u> a deep understanding of other cultures.

In Japan, you <u>shouldn't put</u> a business card in your wallet without studying it first.

To give advice for the past, use this structure:

> should
> ought to   } + have + past participle*
> shouldn't

Example: The company <u>should have known</u> to ask about the customs.

* For a list of irregular past participles, see page 247. Past participles of regular verbs end in *-ed*.

B. Practice. Give advice to George. He's leaving for a fabulous trip around the world. With a partner, make sentences with *should, shouldn't,* or *ought to* + the simple form of the verb. Use the phrases below.

> *Example:* In Taiwan, he should flatter his host.

It's a good idea to:

1. flatter (give compliments to) your host (Taiwan)

2. shake hands when you say "hello" or "good bye" (Italy)

3. learn to bow correctly (Japan)

4. touch your left fingers to your right arm when giving or receiving something (Korea)

5. use the spoon above the plate for dessert (Greece)

It's not a good idea to:

6. refuse an offer of alcohol (Russia)

7. give an even number of flowers (France)

8. eat with your fingers (Turkey)

9. use the American hand signal for "okay" (Brazil)

10. have three people in a photograph (Vietnam)

C. Practice. George has returned from his trip. Poor George! The trip was a disaster because he did absolutely everything wrong. With a partner, make sentences of advice in the past. Use *should(n't) have* or *ought to have* + past participle. Use the phrases in Practice B.

The Subject *You*

The word *you* is, of course, the second person singular and plural. But it has another meaning, too. It can also mean "everyone, people in general."

Example: <u>You</u> should remove <u>your</u> shoes before entering a Thai home.

In *very* formal English, the word *one* has this same meaning of "everyone."

Example: <u>One</u> should remove <u>one's</u> shoes before entering a Thai home.

D. Application.   Think of important customs in your culture. On a piece of paper, write five sentences of advice for people who travel to your country. Use *should(n't)* or *ought to*. Begin with *you*.

Adjective Clauses (Relative Clauses)

You can use an adjective clause to modify (describe) a noun. An adjective clause adds information to a sentence. If the information in the adjective clause is essential, there is no comma before it. An adjective clause might begin with *who* or *that* (for people), *which* or *that* (for things and places), *where* (for places), or *whose* (for possessives). This clause comes immediately after the noun.

Examples: A company <u>that does business internationally</u> ought to have a deep understanding of other cultures.

   (The adjective clause modifies the subject in this sentence, *a company*.)

   The ad listed places <u>where you can buy the product</u>.

   (In this sentence the adjective clause modifies the object, *places*.)

E. Practice.   Find the adjective clause in each sentence. Underline it and draw an arrow (⌒) to the word that it modifies.

1. The first question that an American usually asks a new acquaintance is "What do you do?"

2. A woman who is traveling in the Middle East should not wear short skirts or low-cut blouses.

3. He spent time in three countries where his company did business.

4. In Arab countries, when a man greets another man who has higher status, he should wait until the other man offers to shake hands.

5. Customs that are very different in various cultures involve the use of gestures—hand movements for communication.

F. Sentence Combining: Adjective Clauses.   Combine these pairs of sentences. Make the second sentence in each pair into an adjective clause and add it to the first.

1. A business will probably not be successful.

   A business is culturally insensitive.

   _____

   _____

2. The woman was the new manager.

   The woman called the meeting.

   _____

   _____

3. One custom is going to public baths.

   One custom seems a little unusual to some people.

   _____

   _____

4. We visited an acquaintance.

   The acquaintance's home was just outside the city.

   _____

   _____

5. An American is saying "good luck."

   An American crosses his fingers.

   _____

   _____

6. He went to work for a company.

   The company did a lot of international business.

   _____

   _____

Transitional Expressions: Coordinating Conjunctions

You can join two independent clauses (complete sentences) with a comma and a coordinating conjunction. There are seven coordinating conjunctions. One of them, *nor,* will not be covered in this chapter. These are the other six.

> **and** introduces more information; it adds one idea to another
>
> **but** introduces information that might be surprising, unexpected, or opposite the information in the first clause
>
> **yet** means "but"; it is very formal
>
> **so** means "that's why"
>
> **for** means "because"; it is very formal
>
> **or** introduces another possibility

Examples: U.S. customers believe that Swiss chocolate is especially good, <u>and</u> they buy a lot of it.

Russians believe that McDonald's food is good, <u>so</u> they wait in long lines to eat it.

International businesses need to understand the culture of other countries, <u>or</u> they will probably have difficulty selling their product.

If there isn't an independent clause after the coordinating conjunction, don't use a comma. Usually, this situation happens when the subject in both clauses is the same, and you don't repeat it in the second clause. This is most common with *and.*

Examples: They saw the product, <u>and</u> they liked it.

They saw the product <u>and</u> liked it.

In a series of three or more nouns, adjectives, verbs, or phrases, use commas between each item. This structure occurs with *and* or *or.*

Examples: You should bring flowers, candy, <u>or</u> wine to a dinner party.

The advertisement showed dirty clothes on the left, a box of soap in the middle, <u>and</u> clean clothes on the right.

G. Sentence Combining: Coordinating Conjunctions.   Combine these sentences. Use *and, but, yet, or, for,* or *so.*

1. She had lived in Finland for fifteen years.

She spoke the language fluently.

_____

_____

2. It's a good idea to bring a gift to the hostess.

You shouldn't bring wine if the family doesn't drink alcohol.

_____

_____

3. The company produces cars.

The company produces trucks.

The company produces vans.

_____

_____

4. You need to ask for the bill in a restaurant in Italy.

The waiter won't bring it.

_____

_____

5. In Spain, an older person may use your first name.

You should use "Mr." or "Mrs." and the person's last name.

_____

_____

6. You may have wine.

You may have juice.

You may have water.

_____

_____

7. The company wasn't successful.

It didn't understand the business customs of the country.

_____

_____

8. Most people in that country speak two languages.

Some speak three or four.

_____

_____

. . : : : : **Part Five** Writing in the Academic World

Before Writing

 writing **Strategy**

Brainstorming

Before you write a paragraph, you need ideas. One way to begin getting ideas is to *brainstorm*. When you brainstorm, several people work together and suggest as many ideas as possible. Some of these ideas are general, and some are specific. Some are good ideas, and some might not be very good, but it doesn't matter. In brainstorming, it's important simply to get your ideas on paper. One person in the group writes down *all* of the ideas. Later, you can use this list and choose a topic.

A. Brainstorming.   In small groups, brainstorm the answers to these questions. Choose a "group secretary" to write your answers on a piece of paper.

1. How many cross-cultural mistakes did this chapter include? What were they? (Look back at Parts One, Two, and Four.)

2. Look back at your notes on the Elements of Culture chart on page 22. Now think about foreigners in your country and international companies that do business in your country. What are some common misconceptions that foreigners have of your culture? What mistakes have international companies made in your country?

writing Strategy

Choosing a Topic

In most writing assignments, your teacher will give you some choice of topic, within limits. *It's important for you to choose carefully a topic that you enjoy and have ideas about.*

B. Choosing a Topic.   To prepare for the writing assignment in this chapter, first choose *one* element of culture: language, religion, values, material culture, or customs. Then choose *one* of your examples from your notes on the chart on page 22. You're going to write one paragraph to answer this question:

> What is one thing that multinational businesses should know about your culture?

writing Strategy

Narrowing a Topic

After you choose a topic, you need to narrow it—in other words, make it specific enough to cover well in just one paragraph. The example below is about U.S. culture.

Example: general topic: language

> more specific: the English language
>
> more specific: the importance for immigrants of learning English
>
> more specific: the importance for immigrants of not being shy about practicing English

C. Practice.   For each group, decide which topic is most general, and put a 1 on the line. Which is more specific? Put a 2. Which is the most specific? Put a 3. Only those that you number 3 are probably specific enough to be the topic of a paragraph.

1. _____ a laundry detergent advertisement in Arabic

   _____ advertising

   _____ the problem with a laundry detergent advertisement written in Arabic

2. _____ mistakes in advertisements for McDonald's in Brazil

   _____ advertising in Brazil

   _____ advertisements for McDonald's in Brazil

3. _____ language

   _____ how a knowledge of the local language can help a businessperson

   _____ knowledge of a new language

4. _____ the importance of religion in everyday life

   _____ how religion influences people's work life

   _____ religion

5. _____ ethnocentrism

   _____ ethnocentrism in international organizations

   _____ an example of ethnocentrism in one multinational enterprise

6. _____ understanding customs and manners in other countries

   _____ customs and manners

   _____ why international businesspeople need to understand customs and manners
          of other countries

D. Narrowing Your Topic.   Check your own topic. If it is too general, you need to narrow it as much as possible.

E. Planning. Before you begin to write, make notes about your topic. This is similar to brainstorming, but you do it alone.

1. Write your topic at the top of a piece of paper. Then write anything about this topic that you can think of. Don't write complete sentences. Just write notes.

2. After you write all of your ideas, cross out anything that doesn't belong. A paragraph must be about *one* topic.

    Example: topic: the importance for international enterprises of understanding the diversity of U.S. culture

        ideas: men/~~women~~—equal

             multiethnic society

             ~~not really as equal as we like to think~~

             ~~example of a cross-cultural mistake: sexual harrassment at one company~~

             example of a cross-cultural mistake: advertisement for a multinational car company

Writing

writing Strategy

Writing a Paragraph of Example

A paragraph has one topic (subject). The *topic sentence* is usually the first sentence. It includes the topic and the main idea of the paragraph. It is usually the most general sentence of the paragraph. The other sentences give details—specific information—to support the main idea. *Examples* are one kind of detail. There are two types of paragraphs of example: 1) a paragraph with several short examples to support the topic sentence, and 2) a paragraph with one longer example to support the topic sentence. The example in this box is the second type.

    To write your paragraph, write out the notes that you have prepared in the form of complete sentences.

Example: Multinational companies that do business in the United States shouldn't ignore the importance of diversity in American culture. The United States is a multiethnic society with people from almost every imaginable race, religion, language, and culture. A business that ignores this is probably making a cultural mistake. For example, a car company recently put an advertisement in a national U.S. magazine. In the ad, there were photographs of all the managers of the car dealerships in the country—forty-four of them. They were all smiling and looked friendly, yet there was one problem. They were all white, middle-aged men. There were no women, blacks, Asians, or Native Americans. The implied meaning of this advertisement was clear: only white middle-aged men were welcome customers. The company ignored the majority of the U.S. population, so the majority of the U.S. population ignored the company and didn't buy the car.

Notice these points in the example:

- The first word is indented, and all of the other lines begin at the margin.

- Every sentence begins with a capital letter and ends with a period.

- After a period (.) the next sentence begins on the same line.

- The example supports the main idea.

- The beginning of the paragraph is in the simple present tense because it is about something that is generally true. The example is in the simple past tense because it is from the (recent) past.

Analysis.   In the sample paragraph, look for 1) coordinating conjunctions and 2) adjective clauses. Circle them.

Writing Assignment: First Draft.   Write a paragraph about something that multinational companies should understand about your culture. Be sure to have your topic and main idea in the first sentence. Include an example.

After Writing

A. Self-Check.   Read over your paragraph. Answer the questions on the checklist. Write yes or no.

B. Classmate's Check.   Exchange papers with a classmate. Check each other's paragraphs. Write yes or no on your classmate's checklist.

editing Checklist

Points To Check For	My Check	My Classmate's Check
1. Is the paragraph form correct (indentation, margins)?	_____	_____
2. Does the topic sentence include the topic and main idea?	_____	_____
3. Does the example support the topic sentence?	_____	_____
4. Is the use of coordinating conjunctions correct?	_____	_____
5. If there are adjective clauses, are they used correctly?	_____	_____
6. Is the use of tenses correct?	_____	_____
7. Other: _____	_____	_____

Second Draft.   Use the answers on the checklist to help you rewrite your paragraph. Then give your paragraph to your teacher.

Answers to the Cross-Cultural Business IQ Test (pages 12–13):

1. b   **6.** c

2. c   **7.** b

3. b   **8.** b

4. a   **9.** c

5. b   **10.** b

chapter Two

International Economy

In this chapter, you'll read about cross-cultural business and different economic systems. You'll write about the economic system in your own country.

Part One Supply and Demand—Stories in the News

Before Reading

A. Discussion.   Look at the pictures. With a partner, answer these questions.

1. What is the purpose of military tanks? Why are they not as important as they used to be?

2. Do you have any animals similar to prairie dogs in your country? If so, where do they live? What do they eat? What do people think about them?

a. A farm in the United States

b. A military tank

c. Prairie dogs in the American midwest

B. Thinking Ahead. In small groups, make a list of problems that farmers have. List as many as possible.

Reading

As you read the following passage, think about the answer to this question.

• What are two new businesses that are solving some problems of farmers?

Supply and Demand: Stories in the News

A term that we often use when we talk about business is "supply and demand." **Supply** is the amount of a product or service that is available for people to buy or use. **Demand** is people's
5 desire or need for a product or service. The term **supply and demand** means the balance between the amount for sale and the amount that people want or need. Recent stories in the news offer two unusual examples of how supply and demand
10 functions in the changing world of international business. Coincidentally, both examples begin on farms.

Many farmers in England have been worried in recent years about the future of farming in their
15 country. Prices for farm products have gone down, and taxes on farmland have gone up. Several British farmers have decided to adapt to the changing times. They have changed their ordinary farms (which used to grow crops such as
20 potatoes) into tank farms. *Tank* farms? The farmers noticed that there was an oversupply of military tanks in England because of the end of the Cold War. They bought some tanks and found people to give lessons in tank driving. Now, city
25 people who want a new and unusual experience can spend a weekend on a farm in the country. There, they can learn to drive a tank without hurting anyone or being in a war. The owners of Highlands Park Farm in Wiltshire say that busi-
30 ness is very good.

Thousands of miles away, farmers in the American midwest had a different challenge: prairie dogs. These animals dig deep holes—burrows—where they live and hide. Prairie dogs
35 have always been a problem for farmers because they destroy the farmers' crops. For many years, farmers have tried to kill these animals in different ways, but nothing has worked. In addition, farmers have a problem with animal rights
40 groups, who don't want animals to suffer.

Vacuum cleaner

One man had a strange but successful solution to this problem. He invented a
45 very large vacuum cleaner. It's the size of a truck. He travels around with this huge machine and *vacuums*
50 prairie dogs out of their burrows. The prairie dogs are surprised by this experience, but they aren't hurt. The farmers are happy. And the man with the
55 vacuum truck is doing good business. Farmers pay him for his service, and he makes more money when he sells pairs of prairie dogs to people in Tokyo who think they are cuter pets than dogs or cats.

After Reading

A. Comprehension Check.   Answer these questions with a partner.

1. What problem have many British farmers had?

2. Why did the military have an oversupply of tanks?

3. How did the British farmers solve their problems?

4. What has always been a problem for farmers in the American midwest?

5. What did one man invent to solve the problem?

6. In what two ways does this man now make money?

B. Application.   You've read about two examples of how supply and demand functions. In each example, what was the *supply*? What was the *demand*? Work with a partner to fill in the following chart.

	Supply	Demand
England		
American Midwest / Tokyo		

C. Response Writing.   Choose *one* of these topics.

- problems of farmers in your country

- animals that are popular pets in your country

- your opinion about tank farms in England

- your opinion about vacuuming prairie dogs out of their burrows

- your idea for a new invention

Write about your topic for ten minutes. Don't worry about grammar and don't stop writing to use a dictionary. Just put as many ideas as possible on paper.

 **Part Two** Business in Literature: Excerpt from Lawrence Durrell's *Bitter Lemons*

Before Reading

A. Discussion.   Answer these questions with a partner.

1. In your country, what do people do when they want to buy a house? Do they go directly to the owner of the house, or do they ask a *real estate agent* for help?

2. In what situations can people argue about the price of something? (In a supermarket? A farmers' market? A furniture store?)

3. How are the customs for discussing price different in your country from the United States?

4. Do you know someone who is very good at negotiating and buying things cheaply?

5. The reading passage takes place on the island of Cyprus. Where is Cyprus? What are the nationalities of the people who live there?

reading Strategy

Understanding New Words—Accepting Uncertainty

When you're reading material that seems difficult, you need to guess the meaning of new words, if possible. *It's important to remember that it's okay if you don't understand a word **exactly**.* However, if you cannot guess *anything* about it, you need to learn when to look up the word (in a dictionary) and when not to worry about it.

Examples: He was perhaps forty years of age, <u>sturdily</u> built, and with a fine head on his shoulders. His actions and words <u>flowed</u> from him like honey from a spoon.

"They are all here," he <u>hissed</u>. He pointed to the cafe across the road where the <u>cobbler</u> had gathered his family.

Which new words can you guess from this short piece from Lawrence Durrell's book *Bitter Lemons*? Probably only <u>flowed</u>. You know how honey moves from a spoon, so you can guess that flowed might mean "moved slowly, like a thick liquid." From this context, you have no idea about the meaning of <u>sturdily</u>, but you probably don't need this word in order to understand the passage. Don't look it up. You can guess that <u>hissed</u> means "said" in some specific way, but you don't know the exact meaning. Is it important to know the exact meaning? No, so don't look it up. From this context, you can't guess much about the word <u>cobbler</u>. You see that a cobbler is a person (in this case a man), but you don't know anything else. You probably need a dictionary for this word.

Reading

As you read the following passage by Lawrence Durrell, don't use a dictionary. Decide which new words are important and which ones aren't. You'll practice vocabulary after the reading passage.

A Word to Set the Scene.   In the 1950s, the English writer Lawrence Durrell decided to live on the Mediterranean island of Cyprus for a year or two, where he planned to teach and write. He wanted to buy a house in a village there and went to a Turkish real estate agent for help in this. Together, they found a wonderful old house with great wooden doors and a glorious view of hills, villages, and a distant castle. Durrell wanted the house very, very much but didn't have much money. He needed an especially smart businessman to negotiate the purchase for him from the Greek woman who owned the house. The real estate agent, Sabri Tahir, was famous on the island for his cleverness.

   The following is an excerpt from Lawrence Durrell's book *Bitter Lemons,* about his time on Cyprus. In this scene, Durrell and Sabri Tahir are in Sabri's office. The owner of the house, a shoemaker's wife, is across the street in a cafe with many relatives who are giving her advice. The huge key to the house is on the desk in front of Sabri.

How to Buy a House

[Sabri Tahir] was perhaps forty years of age, sturdily built, and with a fine head on his shoulders. He had the sleepy good looks—a rare smile with perfect teeth, thoughtful brown
5 eyes—which one sees sometimes in Turkish travel posters.

   "They are all here," he hissed. He pointed to the cafe across the road where the cobbler had gathered his family. They sat on a semicircle of
10 chairs, sipping coffee and arguing in low voices. "Now, whatever happens," said Sabri in a low voice, "do not surprise. You must never surprise. And you don't want the house at all, see?"

   I repeated the words, "I don't want the house. I absolutely don't want the house." Yet
15 in my mind's eye I could see those great doors. ("God," Sabri had said, "this is fine wood. From Anatolia. In the old days they floated the great timbers over the water behind boats. This is Anatolian timber, it will last forever.") "I don't want the house," I repeated under my breath.

   [The woman] walked boldly across the road, entering with a loud "Good morning."
20 She wore the white headdress and dark skirt of the village woman.

   Sabri cleared his throat, and picking up the great key very delicately between finger and thumb, put it down again on the edge of the desk nearest her. "We are speaking about your house," he said softly. "Do you know that all the wood is . . ." he suddenly shouted

25 the last word with such force that I nearly fell off my chair, "rotten!" And picking up the key he banged it down to emphasize the point.

The woman threw up her head and taking up the key also banged it down exclaiming: "It is not."

"It *is*." Sabri banged the key.

"It is *not*." She banged it back.

30 "It *is*." A bang.

"It is *not*." A counter bang.

All this was not on a very high intellectual level. I also feared that the key itself would be banged out of shape so that finally none of us would be able to get into the house.

The woman now took the key and held it up as if she were swearing by it. "The house 35 is a good house," she cried. Then she put it back on the desk. Sabri took it up thoughtfully. "And suppose we wanted the house," he said, "which we don't, what would you ask for it?"

"Eight hundred pounds."

Sabri gave a long laugh, wiping away imaginary tears and repeating "Eight hundred pounds" as if it were the best joke in the world. He laughed at me and I laughed at him, 40 a dreadful false laugh. We laughed until we were exhausted. Then we grew serious again. Sabri was still fresh as a daisy, I could see that. He had put himself into the patient state of mind of a chess player. Then he suddenly turned to her. "Two hundred pounds and not a piastre more."

She turned back to Sabri and banging the key down once more shouted "Six hundred."

45 "I offer you two hundred pounds."

She let out a yell. "No. Never in this life."

My friend leaned back in his chair. "Think of it," he said, his voice full of the poetry of commerce. "This gentleman will [write you a check]. You will go to the bank. They will open the safe. They will take from it notes, thick notes, as thick as a honeycomb, as thick 50 as salami." (Here they both licked their lips and I myself began to feel hungry at the thought of so much edible money.) "All you have to do is to agree."

Source: "How to Buy a House" adapted from Lawrence Durrell, *Bitter Lemons,* (New York: E. P. Dutton & Co., 1957). Copyright © 1957 by Lawrence Durrell. Reprinted with the permission of Curtis Brown, Ltd. and Faber and Faber, Ltd.

After Reading

A. Making Inferences.   The people in this scene are talking about business—the sale of a house—but Durrell describes them as if they are actors in a theatrical play. In small groups, discuss these questions.

1. Who is the "star" of this play?

2. What two lies does Sabri tell?

3. From which sentences and paragraphs can you infer that Sabri is acting?

4. What do you think will happen next?

 *reading* Strategy

Understanding Parts of Speech

When you need to use a dictionary, it's a good idea to know the *part of speech* of the word that you're looking up *before you open the dictionary*. What is the reason for this? Many words can have more than one part of speech, so you'll save time if you go directly to the correct part of speech and ignore the others. How can you know the part of speech? Look in the sentence.

Examples: She wore a dark <u>skirt</u>.   (noun)

He <u>skirted</u> the topic for several minutes.   (verb)

If you're looking up the *verb* "skirt," you don't want to waste time reading definitions of the *noun* "skirt."

A dictionary will tell you the part of speech with these abbreviations:

n = noun   v = verb   prep = preposition
adj = adjective   adv = adverb   conj = conjunction

B. Practice.   Decide which part of speech belongs in each blank. Write it in the parentheses. Then write a logical word in that part of speech in the blank. (There might be many possible answers for each blank.) When you finish, compare your answers with another student's.

1. He was famous for his (___n___) _____honesty / cleverness_____ .

2. They opened the (_____) _____ and took out money.

3. She (_____) _____ the key on the desk.

4. We heard a loud (_____) _____ .

5. I looked (_____) _____ the paper.

6. "Look over there," he (_____) _____ .

7. She walked (_____) _____ across the street.

8. He wanted me to (_____) _____ it.

9. It's a (_____) _____ house.

10. He (_____) _____ shouted this word.

C. Practice. Decide the part of speech of each underlined word. Then look it up in a monolingual (English-English) dictionary and write the definition.

1. He <u>banged</u> the key on the table to emphasize his point.

    Part of Speech: _____

    Definition: _____

2. She closed the door with a <u>bang</u>.

    Part of Speech: _____

    Definition: _____

3. The house is strong and well built. It will <u>last</u> forever.

    Part of Speech: _____

    Definition: _____

4. This is my <u>last</u> offer.

    Part of Speech: _____

    Definition: _____

5. They will open the <u>safe</u> and take out the money.

    Part of Speech: _____

    Definition: _____

6. She felt <u>safe</u> in the circle of her family.

    Part of Speech: _____

    Definition: _____

7. The bank teller handed her a thick stack of <u>notes</u>.

    Part of Speech: _____

    Definition: _____

8. Please <u>note</u> that it's important to do this quickly.

    Part of Speech: _____

    Definition: _____

D. Vocabulary Check.   Find a word or expression in the passage for each definition that follows. The numbers in parentheses refer to lines.

1. drinking in small amounts (10–15): _____

2. carried in the water (15–20): _____

3. wood or large wooden beams (15–20): _____

4. carefully, gently (20–25): _____

5. gone bad (20–25): _____

6. promising that one is telling the truth (30–35): _____

7. not real (40–45): _____

8. something that one can eat (adjective) (50–51): _____

reading **Strategy**

Keeping a Word Journal

Keeping a Word Journal is a good way to study, review, and remember new words. Buy a thin spiral notebook and put the label WORD JOURNAL on the front. In it, you will record words that are important for you to remember. All of the students in a class will be working with the same reading passages, but each student might find different words from these passages to put in the journal. Spend ten to twenty minutes each day on this. Include this information.

- the word (or idiom)
- the part of speech
- a synonym or definition (either your guess or from a dictionary)
- a sentence with the word in it

Example: underline{emphasize} (verb)

to put emphasis on; to stress or give special force to something to show that it is especially important

Ex.: He banged down the key to emphasize his point.

E. Word Journal.   Go back to the passage "How to Buy a House." Which new words are important for you to remember? Put them in your Word Journal.

F. Vocabulary Expansion. There are traditional expressions of comparison in every language. Durrell uses one in the passage: *as fresh as a daisy.* (The structure is **as** + adjective + **as** + noun.) On the following chart, there are the beginnings of some traditional expressions in English. How do you think they end? Fill in the missing noun for each one. Write your opinion or the way that people say this in your culture. Then ask two other classmates for their answers.*

	My Noun	**Classmate #1**	**Classmate #2**
1. as busy as . .			
2. as tough as . . .			
3. as free as . . .			
4. as hard as . . .			
5. as soft as . . .			
6. as easy as . . .			
7. as deep as . . .			
8. as pretty as . . .			

* Note: You can find out how to say these in English on page 68.

 reading **Strategy**

Understanding Italics

Writers use *italics* (slanted letters) for different reasons.

• The words in italics are the title of a book, movie, newspaper, or magazine.
• A word in italics might be a foreign word used in an English sentence.
• The writer is using italics to emphasize a word.

G. Practice. Find words in italics in "How to Buy a House." Why did Durrell use italics for these words?

.:.:.:.: **Part Three** Reading in the Academic World

Before Reading

 *reading* Strategy

---

Guessing Meaning from Context

Sometimes you can guess the meaning of a new word from information in the next sentence.

Example: Business doesn't <u>take place</u> on Fridays in that company. For religious reasons, no
business can occur on a Friday.

(Here we see that <u>take place</u> means "occur.")

Often, the next sentence can tell you *something* about a new word but not enough so that you can
guess the exact meaning.

Example: In that country the government owns the <u>factors</u> of production. It has control of the
equipment, work schedules, salaries, and prices.

(In this example, it's impossible to know the exact meaning of <u>factors</u>, but we can
guess, in general, that it means "things that are part of" or "conditions.")

Sometimes you can find the meaning of a new word or expression before or after the phrase *that is*
or *in other words*.

Example: Decisions are based on <u>customs, beliefs, and religion</u>—that is, the traditional way of
doing things.

(We see that <u>customs, beliefs, and religion</u> are the traditional way of doing things.)

A. Vocabulary Preparation.   The following textbook passage has some words that will be new
to you. You don't need a dictionary for some of them because you can guess the meaning from the
context. For other words, you can understand something but not everything. What can you guess about
each underlined word? First, write the part of speech. Then write your guess and compare your answer
with another student's. After that, check with a monolingual dictionary to see if your guess was close.

1. Each society's values and goals <u>determine</u> its economic system. These values and goals decide
   the type of economy for the country.

   Part of Speech: _____

   My Guess: _____

   Dictionary Definition: _____

2. That country is rich in <u>resources</u>. It has oil, minerals, and timber.

Part of Speech: _____

My Guess: _____

Dictionary Definition: _____

3. A variety of <u>goods</u> can be bought at that store. You can buy clothes, furniture, tools, books, and so on.

Part of Speech: _____

My Guess: _____

Dictionary Definition: _____

4. There was a <u>distribution</u> of food and clothing to people of the neighborhood after the hurricane destroyed their homes. The government gave out these necessities to anyone who needed them.

Part of Speech: _____

My Guess: _____

Dictionary Definition: _____

5. That American company wanted to do business in North Korea, but the government <u>intervened</u>. The U.S. government stepped in and prevented this.

Part of Speech: _____

My Guess: _____

Dictionary Definition: _____

6. These people are <u>nomadic</u> hunters and gatherers. In other words, they travel from one area to another to hunt animals and gather fruits and vegetables.

Part of Speech: _____

My Guess: _____

Dictionary Definition: _____

7. The government <u>regulates</u>—that is, controls—the amount of education that people receive.

Part of Speech: _____

My Guess: _____

Dictionary Definition: _____

B. Previewing.   Before you read, look over the following textbook passage, "Economic Systems," very quickly. What are four topics in this passage? Write them here.

1. _____   2. _____

3. _____   4. _____

Reading

As you read the passage, think about the answer to this question.

• How are the four economic systems different from each other?

Economic Systems

Various nations have different economic systems, but each system must answer the same four basic questions: 1) What goods and services (and
5 how much of each) should be produced? 2) Who should produce them? 3) How should they be produced? 4) Who should be able to use them? Each society answers these questions according to its values and goals,
10 which determine its economic system. Economists have identified four types of economic systems: traditional, command (or controlled), market (or capitalist), and mixed.

Traditional System

15 A pure traditional economic system answers the four basic questions according to tradition. In such a system, things are done "the way they have always been done." Economic decisions are based on
20 customs, beliefs, and religion—that is, the traditional way of doing things. The San people of southern Africa, for example, are nomadic hunters and gatherers. In other

words, the San travel from one area to
25 another to hunt animals and gather fruits and vegetables, and they move on when there is no more food. Traditional economic systems exist today in very few areas of Asia, the Middle East, Africa, and Latin
30 America.

Command (or Controlled) System

In a pure command economic system, an individual person has little—or possibly no—influence over how the basic economic questions are answered. The government

and services. This exchange of goods and services may take place in a neighborhood
60 market for someone's services such as delivering newspapers, or it may happen in a worldwide market for a good such as oil. People may take, refuse, or change jobs whenever they want to—if there is a de-
65 mand for their labor.

35 controls production and makes all decisions about the use of goods and services. "The government" may be one person, a small group of leaders, or a group of central planners in a government agency.
40 These people choose how resources will be used and decide the distribution of goods and services. They also regulate—that is, control—the amount of education that people receive, so they guide people into
45 certain jobs. These days, the only areas that still have a pure command economy are North Korea and parts of China.

Market (or Capitalist) System

The opposite of a pure command economic system is a pure market economic sys-
50 tem—or capitalism, in which the government does not intervene. In other words, individual people own the factors of production, and they decide for themselves the answers to the four basic economic
55 questions. Economic decisions are made in the market—that is, the freely chosen activity between buyers and sellers of goods

Mixed System

Except for the traditional economic system, a *pure* economic system has probably never existed; most economies are mixed. A mixed economy has some characteristics
70 of a command economy and some of a market economy. Two examples are the United States and the People's Republic of China. The U.S. economy tends toward the market system, but there are laws that
75 regulate some areas of business. The People's Republic of China tends toward the command system, but in some "special economic zones" people can make economic decisions without interference by the
80 government.

Source: "Economic Systems" adapted from Roger LeRoy Miller, *Economics: Today and Tomorrow*, pp. 30–35. Copyright © 1995, 1991 Glencoe/McGraw-Hill. Reprinted with the permission of the publishers.

After Reading

reading Strategy

Marking a Book

In college, students need to do a huge amount of reading, and there usually isn't enough time to read a chapter several times. You need to learn to mark the important information in a reading passage so that you can find it quickly later. One way to do this is to use a felt-tip marking pen—bright yellow, green, or orange—to catch the eye easily.

A. Main Ideas.

1. Look back at the first paragraph of the textbook passage. Which sentence is a "map" that tells you what to expect in the rest of the passage? Highlight it with a felt-tip pen.

2. Now look at the second, third, and fourth paragraphs. If you could choose just *one* sentence to remember from each of these paragraphs, which one would it be? Highlight it with a felt-tip pen. Then compare your answers with another student's.

B. Comprehension Check.   On a piece of paper, write the four economic systems and give a definition of each.

C. Vocabulary Check.   Find a word or expression in the passage for each definition that follows. The numbers in parentheses refer to lines.

1. people who study economics (10–15): _____

2. command economy (30–35): _____

3. market economy (45–50): _____

4. to show the way or tell someone where to go (40–45): _____

5. the freely chosen activity between buyers and sellers of goods and services (55–60): _____

6. everywhere in the world (60–65): _____

7. work (noun) (65–70): _____

8. "leans" in one direction instead of another (70–75): _____

D. Vocabulary Expansion.

Your vocabulary will grow faster if you learn different parts of speech when you learn a new word. Use the textbook passage and a dictionary to fill in these blanks.

Verb	Noun	Adjective
1. determine	_____	_____
2. X	_____	nomadic
3. _____	distribution	_____
4. regulate	_____	_____
5. tend	_____	X

Stretch Your Vocabulary!

If *worldwide* means "everywhere in the world," what do you think these words mean?

nationwide	schoolwide
statewide	countrywide
citywide	campuswide

E. Discussion.

In small groups, answer these questions.

1. What is the economic system in your country? If you have a mixed economy, does it tend to be more command or market? What does the government regulate?

2. What is the effect of religious beliefs and values on your country's economy? What effect does religion have on the economy of other countries?

3. Look back at the reading passages in Parts One and Two. What economic system are these people working in? How do you know?

F. Application.   Imagine this situation. You were on a ship that sank very close to an uninhabited island; that is, nobody lives there. Everyone safely reached the island from the ship, but there wasn't an opportunity to take anything from the ship. You and the other people need to be calm and well-organized because it's possible that you will be on this island for *ten years*. The island is rich in natural resources and has many kinds of plants and animals, but the only source of drinking water is high on top of a hill, one mile away from the best place to build a village.

Work in small groups to apply your knowledge of economic systems to the problem of surviving on this island. How would each system answer the four basic economic questions to organize life on the island? Fill in the following chart.

Economic Systems

Basic Economic Questions	Traditional	Command	Market	Mixed
What goods and services should be produced?				
Who should produce them?				
How should they be produced?				
Who should be able to use them?				

. .:::: **Part Four** The Mechanics of Writing

In Part Five, you are going to write about the economic system in one country. In your paragraph, you may need to use the passive voice and adverbial conjunctions. Part Four will help you to understand and use these grammar points.

The Passive Voice

We often use the passive voice instead of the active voice if the subject (in the active voice) is *obvious, unnecessary,* or *unknown.*

Examples: Farmers <u>grow</u> potatoes on that farm. (active voice)

Potatoes <u>are grown</u> on that farm. (passive voice)

(It's obvious that *farmers* grow crops. The passive voice is better than the active voice in this case.)

People <u>sold</u> the prairie dogs in Tokyo. (active voice)

The prairie dogs <u>were sold</u> in Tokyo. (passive voice)

(The word *people* doesn't add much information to the active voice sentence, so this is a good place to use the passive voice instead.)

In the passive voice, the object (from the active voice) is moved into the subject position.

Example: People have always done <u>this</u> in the same way.   (active voice)
                                                    (object)

<u>This</u> has always been done in the same way.   (passive voice)
(subject)

The passive voice consists of the verb *be* and the past participle of another verb. The verb *be* can be in most tenses or have a modal.

Examples: is done

was done

will be done

has been done

should be done

Note: You'll learn more about the passive voice in Chapter Six.

A. Practice.   Change these active voice sentences to the passive voice. Use the same tense as in the active voice. (The object is underlined.)

1. People base <u>economic decisions</u> on tradition.

    _____

2. People exchanged <u>oil</u> for wheat.

    _____

3. Everyone will need <u>a lot of natural resources</u>.

    _____

4. Someone may offer <u>him</u> a job.

    _____

5. People make <u>economic decisions</u> in the market.

    _____

6. People do <u>things</u> in the same way people have always done <u>them</u>. (Change both parts of the sentence.)

    _____

Transitional Expressions: Adverbial Conjunctions

Transitional expressions carry an idea from one sentence to another and show relationships between sentences. They pull the paragraph together and help the ideas to flow smoothly and logically.

One type of transitional expression is an adverbial conjunction. An adverbial conjunction joins two independent clauses.* There is a period or semicolon before the adverbial conjunction. There is a comma after it (except for *then*).

Examples: The Cold War finally came to an end. <u>Therefore</u>, the military had an oversupply of unnecessary equipment such as tanks.

The farmer didn't want prairie dogs on his land; <u>however</u>, he didn't want to kill or hurt them.

* Note: An independent clause is a group of words that can stand alone. In other words, with a capital letter at the beginning and a period at the end, an independent clause is a sentence.

Here are some of the many adverbial conjunctions, in groups according to meaning.

Adverbial Conjunctions	Meaning
in addition moreover also furthermore	added information (= *and*)
however nevertheless } (Use with a surprising situation.) even so	contradiction (= *but*)
therefore consequently as a result for this (that) reason	cause and effect (= *so* or *that's why*)
for example for instance e.g. (= for example)	example
in other words that is i.e. (= in other words)	explanation, definition (the same information in different words)
next finally then (no comma)	time relationships
mostly for the most part to some extent (= partly) to a large extent (= mostly)	degree (how much)
in short	conclusion, summary

B. Sentence Combining: Adverbial Conjunctions.   Combine the following pairs of sentences. Choose an adverbial conjunction from the group in parentheses.

1. The house had a spectacular view of hills and the sea. It had beautiful wooden doors from Anatolian timber. (added information)

_____

_____

2. They discussed the sale of the house for hours and hours. They agreed on a price. (time relationship)

_____

_____

3. Sabri Tahir was famous for his cleverness in business. Durrell asked him for help in buying a house. (cause and effect)

_____

_____

4. He desperately wanted to own the house. It was important for him to appear completely uninterested in it. (contradiction)

_____

_____

5. Durrell describes Sabri Tahir as having "an air of reptilian concentration and silence." Sabri was able to sit for a long time without moving or speaking but instead just *watched*. (explanation)

_____

_____

6. There were people of different nationalities living in the village. They got along well without many problems. (degree)

_____

_____

C. Sentence Combining. Combine the following pairs of sentences. Choose a logical adverbial conjunction for each.

1. For many years the country had a socialist economy. Now it has a capitalist economy.

_____

_____

2. Religion can have a powerful effect on people's lives. It can influence their attitude toward work.

_____

_____

3. The taxes on their farm were very high, and they weren't getting good prices for their crops. They sold the farm and moved to the city.

_____

_____

4. She studied the language of the country that she was going to live in. She learned as much as possible about the culture.

_____

_____

5. The demand for that book is greater than the supply. There are more people who want to buy the book than there are copies of it.

_____

_____

Avoiding and Repairing Run-Ons and Comma Splices

A common mistake in written (but not spoken) English is the incorrect combination of two sentences.

Example: WRONG: My uncle is losing money on his business he refuses to sell it.

This is incorrect because two independent clauses are combined with no punctuation. The problem is between "business" and "he." This mistake is called a **run-on sentence** because it runs on and on when it should stop.

Sometimes a student tries to "fix" a run-on sentence with a comma.

Example: WRONG: My uncle is losing money on his business, he refuses to sell it.

This does not improve the sentence. It simply replaces one mistake with another. A comma alone cannot hold two independent clauses together. This mistake is called a **comma splice.**

There are several ways to repair a run-on sentence or comma splice. Here are some.

1. Simply separate the two clauses with either a semicolon or a period followed by a capital letter.

   Examples: My uncle is losing money on his business; he refuses to sell it.

   My uncle is losing money on his business. He refuses to sell it.

In many cases—especially if there is *contradiction, cause and effect,* or an *example*—it's more logical, and the style is better, if you use a conjunction. (See #2 and 3 which follow.)

2. Use a comma and a coordinating conjunction. (For a list of coordinating conjunctions, see page 28.)

   Example: My uncle is losing money on his business, but he refuses to sell it.

3. Use a period or semicolon and an adverbial conjunction with a comma after it.

   Example: My uncle is losing money on his business; however, he refuses to sell it.

D. Recognizing and Repairing Run-On Sentences and Comma Splices.   Identify each item as a run-on (R), comma splice (CS), or good sentence (OK). (Hint: look for the place where the two sentences meet.) Then correct the run ons and comma splices. Do not change the good sentences.

_____   1. These people are hunter-gatherers they hunt animals for meat and gather fruits and vegetables.

_____   2. The tribe hunts and gathers in one area they move on when there is no more food.

_____   3. Each person in the tribe has a job to do, the young girls find water and firewood.

_____ **4.** Men do most of the hunting women do most of the gathering.

_____ **5.** Old people in the tribe give advice and look after small children.

_____ **6.** Most hunter-gatherers have some communication with other cultures, the Mbuti Pygmies of Zaire sell hunted meat to their neighbors and buy vegetables.

_____ **7.** There is usually a lot of diversity in the diet the people are generally healthy.

_____ **8.** Hunter-gatherers tend to live in small groups of families that are closely related.

_____ **9.** The people share food with everyone in the group, nobody has to go hungry.

_____ **10.** Hunter-gatherers usually travel from place to place some groups live in large villages.

.::::: **Part Five** Writing in the Academic World

Before Writing

writing Strategy

Writing a Topic Sentence

The topic sentence is usually the first sentence in a paragraph. The topic sentence must be limited and specific enough to develop in one paragraph, but it shouldn't be *too* specific. The topic sentence has two functions: it gives the **topic** of the paragraph, and it says something about this topic. What it says about the topic is the **controlling idea.**

Examples: Many farmers in England have been worried, in recent years, about the future of farming in their country.

Topic: farmers in England

Controlling Idea: have been worried about the future of farming

In a pure command economic system, an individual person has little—or possibly no—influence over how the basic economic questions are answered.

Topic: a pure command economic system

Controlling Idea: an individual person has little or no influence

A topic sentence should not be vague—that is, unclear. Stay away from such words as these: *good, bad, interesting, nice, fun,* and *exciting.*

A. Practice.   Choose the best topic sentence in each group. After you choose, circle the topic and underline the controlling idea. Then decide what is wrong with the other sentences.

1. *a.* It's fun to learn another language.

    b. Knowledge of another language is important.

    c. Knowledge of the local language can help an international businessperson in four ways.

2. *a.* Religion can have a powerful effect on people's work habits.

    b. There are five major religions in the world: Hinduism, Buddhism, Judaism, Christianity, and Islam.

    c. Religion is important in our lives.

3. *a.* Albania has an interesting culture.

    b. It's expensive to travel to Albania.

    c. For many years, Albania had a strict command economy, but this has changed enormously since the end of the Cold War.

4. *a.* Politeness is important in Japan.

    b. International businesspeople who work in Japan need to understand that "yes" doesn't always mean "yes."

    c. It's difficult for international businesspeople to understand Japanese culture.

5. *a.* Life was hard in Russia.

    b. After living in a mostly command economy for decades, Russians are now adapting to a mixed economy that tends toward capitalism.

    c. My grandmother once stood in line for three hours to buy a pair of shoes.

B. Practice.   The following sentences are poor topic sentences. They are too general or don't have a controlling idea. Rewrite each one and make it into a better topic sentence. When you finish, compare your sentences with another student's. (Note: There are many possible answers.)

1. Business is an important subject.

   _____

   _____

2. International businesspeople have many problems.

_____

_____

3. It's good to learn about other cultures.

_____

_____

4. There's a lot of unemployment in my country.

_____

_____

5. Farming is hard work for many reasons.

_____

_____

C. Choosing a Topic. You are going to write a paragraph about the economic system in one country. Look over the questions in the Gathering Information exercise (D). If you can answer most of these questions about your own country, then you'll probably choose to write about the economic system in your country. If you have difficulty with these questions, interview another student; use that person's answers and write a paragraph about his or her country's economic system.

D. Gathering Information. Answer these questions about your country or interview another student about his or her country.

Questionnaire

1. Who decides what a farmer will grow?

   ☐ the farmer

   ☐ a group of farmers

   ☐ the government

   ☐ other: _____

2. Who decides what a factory will produce?

☐ the factory owner(s)

☐ the workers

☐ the government

☐ other: _____

3. Who is able to receive and use goods and services?

☐ anyone who has enough money

☐ anyone who needs them

☐ anyone who works

☐ other: _____

4. Do some people have more goods and services than others?

☐ yes

☐ no

5. How do people choose their profession?

☐ People decide for themselves.

☐ The government chooses it for them.

☐ Tradition tells them to do the same work that their parents did.

☐ other: _____

6. If people are not able to take care of themselves, who takes care of them?

☐ nobody

☐ family members

☐ the village or town or a religious group

☐ the government

☐ a combination (specify: _____)

7. Does the government have laws to regulate conditions in factories?

☐ yes

☐ no

8. Does the government regulate the quality of food, medicine, clothing, or building materials?

☐ yes

☐ no

9. Is there anything that is illegal to grow, produce, buy, or sell?

   ☐ yes (If so, what?) _____

   ☐ no

10. Who owns the airlines, railroads (trains), and buses?

    ☐ private companies

    ☐ the government

    ☐ a combination (both private companies and the government)

11. How is the price determined for things such as food and clothing?

    ☐ The market determines the price.

    ☐ The government sets the price.

    ☐ other: _____

12. How is rent or the price of houses determined?

    ☐ by the market

    ☐ by the government

13. What determines how people work and who does it?

    ☐ the market

    ☐ the government

    ☐ tradition

14. Look at your answers for 1–13. The answers should lead you to the answer to this question: What economic system does your country have?

    ☐ traditional

    ☐ command

    ☐ market

    ☐ mixed

15. If your country has a mixed economy, does it tend toward a command economy or a market economy?

    ☐ command

    ☐ market

Writing

writing Strategy

Developing a Paragraph of Analysis/Organizing Supporting Material

A paragraph of analysis looks at the elements (the basic parts) of something: a poem, an event, a person, a building, a plan, an organization, etc. The supporting sentences focus on each part. They give specific information about the topic sentence. The supporting sentences are more specific than the topic sentence, but there are different levels of specificity. (In other words, some supporting sentences are more specific than others.) A plan of a paragraph of analysis might look like this:

topic sentence

> supporting information
> (about the topic sentence)

>> specific detail
>> (about the supporting information)

> supporting information
> (about the topic sentence)

>> specific detail
>> (about the supporting information)

>>> very specific detail

>>> very specific detail

concluding sentence

In a real paragraph, there would probably be more information and more details than in this diagram. Notice the organization in the paragraph that follows.

Example: In Alaska, the Native people—Indians and Inuit (Eskimos)—have a mixed economic system. For the most part, it is a traditional economy. The people are hunter-gatherers, so economic decisions are based on traditional beliefs and customs. Tradition determines how people hunt and fish and who should do certain jobs; for example, in late summer families go fishing for salmon in the Yukon River. The men and boys catch the fish. The women and girls work together to cut, dry, and smoke the fish. The older people give advice. The fish is distributed to all members of the group. However, the Native people of modern Alaska are also part of the market economy. They have modern houses, engines for their boats, and snowmobiles. To buy these goods, they need to do business in the worldwide market, so they sell fish to Japan and furs to Europe. In addition, the Native Alaskan system has one characteristic of a command economy: state laws and U.S. laws regulate the use of the land and wildlife. In short, the economy of Native Alaskans is traditional but has elements of both capitalism and government control.

Notice the following in the example:

- One of the details is an example.

- The concluding sentence is very similar to the topic sentence but in other words.

In this paragraph (but certainly not in all paragraphs), the concluding sentence includes all three pieces of supporting information.

Understanding Structure.   Look again at the sample paragraph. Find five adverbial conjunctions. Underline them and notice how they are used.

Writing Assignment: First Draft.   Write a paragraph about the economic system in your country or in a classmate's country. Use your answers on the questionnaire as a guide, but *you probably won't use all of your answers.* Also, you might include information that is not on the questionnaire. Be sure to

- have a topic sentence and a concluding sentence.

- have supporting information about the topic sentence.

- have details about the supporting information.

After Writing

A. Self-Check.   Read over your paragraph. Answer the questions on the checklist. Write yes or no.

B. Classmate's Check.   Exchange papers with a classmate. Check each other's paragraphs. Write yes or no on your classmate's checklist.

editing Checklist

Points To Check For	My Check	My Classmate's Check
1. Is the paragraph form correct (indentation, margins)?	_____	_____
2. Does the topic sentence include the country and economic system?	_____	_____
3. Does the supporting information support the topic sentence?	_____	_____
4. Are there details about the supporting information?	_____	_____
5. Is the concluding sentence similar to topic sentence but in different words?	_____	_____
6. Is the use of coordinating and adverbial conjunctions correct?	_____	_____
7. Have run ons and comma splices been avoided?	_____	_____
8. Other: _____	_____	_____

Second Draft.   Use the answers on the checklist to help you to rewrite your paragraph. Then give your paragraph to your teacher.

Answers from page 47, Exercise F. In English these expressions are

1. as busy as a bee   **5.** as soft as silk

2. as tough as leather (nails)   **6.** as easy as pie (1, 2, 3 / A, B, C)

3. as free as a bird   **7.** as deep as the ocean

4. as hard as nails   **8.** as pretty as a picture

Art

chapter Three

Themes and Purposes

In this chapter, you'll learn how to look at art. Specifically, you'll learn about two forms of art—religious and genre. And you'll write a paragraph of comparison-contrast about two paintings.

. : : : : **Part One** Looking at Art: What's the Story?

Before Reading

A. Discussion.   Look at the mysterious figure below. In small groups, answer these questions.

1. Is this a man or a woman?

2. What is the figure doing?

3. What might the figure be made of?

4. How do you think it was made?

5. What condition is it in?

In your opinion, what is this figure?

a. a medicine container

b. a flower vase

c. an anthropomorphic (human-form) perfume jar

d. an anthropomorphic figure to hold an offering to a god or to burn incense

e. a waiter carrying a bowl of soup

B. Thinking Ahead.   Look over the pictures on pages 74–76. Which one do you like the most? Why? Do you know something about any of these pieces of art?

Reading

As you read the following passage, think about the answer to this question.

• What are two ways to look at art?

Looking at Art: What's the Story?

People without much experience in art often do not know what to look for in a work of art. They might glance quickly at a painting or sculpture and decide immediately if they like it or not. In a museum, they hurry past much of the art and, unfortunately, miss out on a lot. However, students of art learn to look at art in two
5 special ways: they use *art criticism* and *art history*. Each has four steps.

In art criticism, students learn first to **describe** the work of art. (What people and things are in the work? What are the details, colors, lines, shapes, and space relationships?) Then they **analyze** the work. (How are the various parts organized?) After that, they **interpret** it. (What feelings, moods, and ideas does the art commu-
10 nicate?) Finally, they **judge** it. (Is it a successful work of art?)

Art history allows students to learn the story behind the work of art. When, where, and by whom was it made? What is the style? How was the artist influenced by the world around him or her? How important is the work?

Let's look back at the figure on page 72 from an art-criticism approach. What
15 might an art critic say? This is an anthropomorphic figure that is carrying a bowl in the right hand. The top of the head also seems to be a bowl. The figure is made of clay. Although it has a human form, it does not look natural. There are two tiny arms and no legs. Instead, the body of the figure is round, shaped almost like a cylinder. We know that it was broken at one time because there are crack marks.

20 An art historian can add the story behind this mysterious figure: it was found in Israel, with many other broken figures, and is about 2,600 years old. It either burned incense or held a religious offering to a god of the Edomite people. Possibly, it was broken in the seventh century BC when King Josiah ordered his soldiers to destroy the culture of "pagan"—that is, non-Jewish—religions.

25 The story behind the work—in other words, art history—can enrich our understanding and enjoyment of art.

Sources: "Looking at Art: What's the Story" adapted, in part, from Gene A. Mittler, *Art in Focus,* pp. 97–99. Copyright © 1994 by Glencoe/ McGraw-Hill. Reprinted with the permission of the publishers. Also adapted, in part, from *Biblical Archaeology Review,* 22, no. 4, (July/ August 1996): pp. 45–48. Copyright © 1996 by Biblical Archaeology Society. Reprinted with the permission of the publishers. *Biblical Archaeology Review* is published on a bimonthly basis. For subscription information, contact *Biblical Archaeology Review* subscriptions, P.O. Box 7026, Red Oak, IA 51591. Subscriptions are currently $14.97 for one year (6 issues), and $26.95 for two years (12 issues).

After Reading

 *reading* Strategy

Determining Point of View

Determining a writer's point of view (opinion, way of looking at a subject) is similar to the skill of making inferences. It helps a reader to understand a passage on a deeper level.

A. Point of View.   According to the passage, there are two ways to look at art. Which one does the writer seem to prefer? Why do you think so?

B. Application.   In small groups, discuss each of these pieces of art (pages 74–76) from the point of view of art criticism; that is, discuss what you see. Then fill in the chart on page 76. Use a dictionary if necessary. If someone in your group knows about the history of the piece (the story behind it), that person should explain it to the others.

1.

2.

3.

4.

5.

Piece of Art	List the people, things, and shapes.	What feeling or mood does it communicate?	What is your opinion of it?	Do you know its history?
1.				
2.				
3.				
4.				
5.				

When you finish, turn to page 106 to find the story behind each piece of art.

⠿ Part Two Art in the Service of Religion

Before Reading

A. Vocabulary Preparation.   The following passage has some words that may be new to you. What can you guess about each underlined word that follows? First, write the part of speech. Then write your guess on the line and compare your answer with another student's.

1. In her history class, she studied the <u>events</u> that took place before the war. Five important things had happened.

   Part of Speech: _____

   My Guess: _____

2. Today, most ancient Greek buildings are white stone, but two thousand years ago they were brightly painted. If you look very closely at some of them, however, you'll notice that a small amount of paint is still <u>visible</u>.

   Part of Speech: _____

   My Guess: _____

3. When he's alone, high up in the mountains, he sometimes gets a very <u>spiritual</u> feeling. There is no church or temple, but he feels that God is all around him.

   Part of Speech: _____

   My Guess: _____

4. We will look at three <u>faiths</u>—the old Greek religion, Buddhism, and Christianity.

   Part of Speech: _____

   My Guess: _____

5. When he thought about his success in business, his large house and expensive car, he felt proud. He sometimes worried a little, however, that this feeling of <u>pride</u> might be dangerous.

   Part of Speech: _____

   My Guess: _____

6. Jews, Christians, and Muslims believe in and honor just one god, but Hindus <u>worship</u> many
gods.

Part of Speech: _____

My Guess: _____

7. She moved her hand in a <u>gesture</u> that meant "look over there."

Part of Speech: _____

My Guess: _____

B. Thinking Ahead.   Think of the religion(s) in your country. Now imagine the art that is an
important part of the religion.

Reading

As you read the passage, think about the answer to this question.

- Why is art important in religion?

_____

Art in the Service of Religion

Since earliest times, art has served religion. Art attempts to take something
invisible, something spiritual, and
make it visible; art gives people images of
5 the people, stories, and events of their faith.
It has been adapted for different purposes
and different religions in different parts of
the world. Here, we will look at art from
three faiths—the old Greek religion, Bud-
10 dhism, and Christianity.

   The first illustration is an example of
religious art from ancient Greece. It is a
sculpture by Praxiteles of the goddess
Aphrodite. To modern eyes, this seems a
15 strange kind of religious statue—a beautiful
nude woman. If we are going to understand
this work of art, we must know something
about the Greek gods. The gods and goddesses of ancient Greece were stronger than
20 humans, and they had powers that humans

Aphrodite of Cnidians, Vatican Museums, Rome

do not have. However, they also had many human characteristics—pride, anger, jealousy, and yes—sexuality. In this context Aphrodite, the goddess of love and beauty,
25 was shown in the nude, and with a body as lovely as the great sculptor could make it. The Greeks worshiped her for her beauty.

Our next two examples, one Buddhist and one Christian, are very different from
30 each other in content. It may be surprising, however, that they are very similar in *form.* The works were created at about the same time but four thousand miles apart.

An image from Tibet shows the Buddha
35 sitting in meditation. He is the largest figure and faces front. His hands are in a classic *mudra*—a hand position that symbolizes the giving of gifts. Around him are *bodhisattvas*—people who have postponed their goal
40 of *Nirvana* (freedom from the cycle of birth, death, and rebirth) because they want to help other people to reach that goal. All of the figures wear halos—golden circles of light around their heads.

45 In the second example, by the thirteenth century Italian master Cimabue, the Virgin Mary, the mother of Christ, is the central figure. She is holding her son, Jesus. Mary is sitting on her throne, with her hand
50 in a gesture toward the Christ child, who is the hope of the world. On both sides of her are angels. These angels are beings who help humans to reach heaven. Again, all of the figures wear halos. Again, the Virgin is the
55 largest figure because she is the most important.

From these pieces of art of three very different religions, we have examples of how artists can make religion more concrete—
60 more real—to believers.

A Tathagata Buddha from Tibet, 13th century

Madonna Enthroned by Cimabue,
Uffizi, Florence

Source: "Art in the Service of Religion" adapted from Rita Gilbert, *Living With Art, Fourth Edition*, pp. 47 and 49–50. Copyright © 1994 by Rita Gilbert. Reprinted with the permission of McGraw-Hill, Inc.

After Reading

A. Main Idea.   Which sentence gives the main idea of the passage? Highlight it with a felt-tip pen.

B. Vocabulary Check.   Find a word in the passage for each definition that follows. The numbers in parentheses refer to lines.

1. an adjective for something that you can't see (1–5):   _____

2. pictures (1–5):   _____

3. a figure (of a person, animal, or thing)
   in stone, wood, etc. (10–15):   _____

4. without clothes (15–20):   _____

5. the subject of a piece of art (30–35):   _____

6. deep and serious thinking, possibly about
   something spiritual (35–40):   _____

7. golden circles of light around the head of a very
   spiritual being (40–45):   _____

8. a chair for a queen or king (45–50):   _____

9. a place of complete happiness; where God lives (50–55):   _____

10. real (55–60):   _____

C. Understanding Italics.   Work with a partner to answer these questions.

1. Which words are in italics in the third and fourth paragraphs?

2. Why are these words in italics? (Check the reasons for italics on page 47, if necessary.)

3. What is the meaning of each italicized word in the fourth paragraph?

reading Strategy

Understanding Pronouns

It's important to understand the meaning of subject pronouns (such as *he, she, it, they*) and object pronouns (such as *him, her, it, them*). Each pronoun refers to a noun or noun phrase before it. Writers use pronouns because they want to avoid repeating a noun.

Examples: The gods and goddesses of ancient Greece were stronger than humans, and <u>they</u> had powers that humans do not have.

    (<u>they</u> = the gods and goddesses of ancient Greece)

    Art takes something invisible and spiritual and makes <u>it</u> visible.

    (<u>it</u> = something invisible and spiritual)

D. Practice.   What does the pronoun mean in each context below? Write the meaning on the line.

1. The first illustration is an example of religious art from Ancient Greece. <u>It</u> is a sculpture of the goddess Aphrodite.

   it = _____

2. The gods and goddesses had powers that humans do not have. However, <u>they</u> also had many human characteristics.

   they = _____

3. Aphrodite was shown in the nude, with a body as lovely as the great sculptor could make it. The Greeks worshiped <u>her</u> for her beauty.

   her = _____

4. The second painting is of the Virgin Mary, the mother of Christ. <u>She</u> is holding her son, Jesus.

   she = _____

E. Vocabulary Expansion.   Your vocabulary will grow faster if you learn different parts of speech when you learn a new word.

1. Use a dictionary, if necessary, to help you fill in these blanks.

Noun	Adjective
pride	_____
anger	_____
jealousy	_____
sexuality	_____

2. Use a dictionary to help you complete this chart about some of the major world religions.

Noun (Religion)	Adjective	Noun (Person Who Believes)
Buddhism	_____	_____
Hinduism	_____	_____
Judaism	_____	_____
Christianity	_____	_____
Islam	_____	_____

F. Discussion.   In small groups, discuss these questions.

1. What is the main religion in your country? Are other religions also important in your country? If so, what are they?

2. What kind of religious art can you find in your culture? (Sculpture? Paintings? Architecture?) What are some topics of this art? Does this art make the religion more visible? If so, how?

G. Finding Similarities and Differences.   Work in small groups to find the similarities and differences between the painting of Buddha from Tibet and the painting of the Virgin Mary from Italy. Look back at the illustrations and reread the fourth and fifth paragraphs Write your answers here.

Similarities:

_____

_____

_____

_____

_____

_____

Differences:

_____

_____

_____

_____

_____

_____

Part Three Reading in the Academic World

Before Reading

A. Vocabulary Preparation.
The following textbook passage has some words that will be new to you. You can understand something about many of them from the context. What can you guess about each underlined word? Write your guess for each word. Then compare your answers with another student's.

1. In their paintings, many artists <u>depict</u> subjects that are close to their personal world.

   My Guess: _____

2. Sometimes an artist's purpose in a painting is to <u>record</u> an important event so that nobody can forget it.

   My Guess: _____

3. Often, political or social <u>issues</u> are depicted in art. Then people discuss these important points for a long time.

   My Guess: _____

4. In our art class, we studied <u>masterpieces</u> of architecture such as the Taj Mahal and masterpieces of painting such as the *Mona Lisa.*

   My Guess: _____

5. The writer lost several pages of her <u>manuscript</u>, so she had to rewrite them before she sent the book to her publisher.

   My Guess: _____

6. The experience lasted for only an <u>instant</u>, and then it was gone.

   My Guess: _____

7. He's one of the thousands of <u>commuters</u> who take the train each day to work in the city and then back home in the evening.

   My Guess: _____

B. Thinking Ahead.
Before you read, look over the four pieces of art on pages 84–87. What is happening in each one?

Reading

As you read the passage, think about the answer to this question.

• What is *genre,* and what is its purpose?

When you find the answer, mark it with a felt-tip pen.

Art as the Mirror of Everyday Life

When children start to draw and paint, they deal with the images that they know best: mother and father, sisters and brothers, the teacher, the house, the dog. Many artists never lose their interest in everyday things, so much of our finest art depicts subjects that are close to the artist's personal world.

Court Ladies Preparing Newly Woven Silk, from China, 12th century

5   Art that depicts the little moments of everyday life and its surroundings is known as *genre.* Often, its purpose is a simple one—to record, to please the eye, to make us smile. Images like this occur in all periods of the history of art, in all cultures and parts of the world. A charming example from China is *Court Ladies Preparing Newly Woven Silk.* No grand political or social issues are presented here. Instead, the artist has depicted a de-
10 lightful scene of daily activity: Three women and a girl stretch and iron a piece of silk, while a little girl peeks underneath to see what is going on. The women's pastel kimonos, their quiet gestures, and the atmosphere of pleasant shared work give us a gentle masterpiece of Chinese genre.

Equally charming genre pieces occur in an early French manuscript, one page of
15 which we shall study here. During the Middle Ages (about 1100–1500 AD), wealthy people
paid artists to illuminate (hand-paint) books, especially prayer books. In the early fifteenth
century, the Limbourg Brothers illuminated one of the most famous books in the history
of art, *Les Très Riches Heures* ("the very rich book of hours"). It contains a calendar, with
each month's painting showing a seasonal activity.

"February" page
from *Les Très
Riches Heures
du Duc de Berry.*
Illumination.
Musee Conde,
Chantilly.

20   The "February" page, shown here, depicts a small hut with three people around a fire.
They have pulled their clothes back to get maximum warmth from the fire. Outside this
small house, we see a snow-covered landscape. There are sheep and birds and three men.
One man is rushing toward the hut with his cloak over his face to keep in the warm breath.
Another man is chopping wood. The third is walking up a hill with a donkey. In the back-
25 ground there is a church.

French artists of another period were also interested in painting life's little moments—
the brief experiences that last for an instant and then are gone. This subject was a favorite
of the Impressionist painters of the late nineteenth century. In Renoir's *Le Moulin de la
Galette,* young couples meet at an outdoor cafe, they dance, they fall in love. We have a
30 quick impression of a delightful way to spend a summer day. We can almost hear the bright
music, feel the warm breezes, and sense an atmosphere of fun.

Renoir's *Le Moulin de la Galette.* 1876

Everyday life in the late twentieth century may take on a different kind of quality, as
we can see in the sculptures of George Segal. In 1982, Segal set up three of his life-size
figures in a New York City bus terminal, as if they were waiting in line to buy a ticket. The
35 figures are naturalistic, but they are made of unpainted white plaster. And they wait. Pa-
tiently, forever, they wait in line, similar to modern-day people who have to wait for so many
small, everyday problems to be solved. Segal, himself a commuter, created what is for city
people, unfortunately, a true mirror of everyday life.

George Segal's
Next Departure.
1979. Installation
1982 at Port
Authority of New
York and New
Jersey Bus Ter-
minal, New York

Source: "Art as the Mirror of Everyday Life" adapted from Rita Gilbert, *Living With Art, Fourth Edition,* pp. 60–63, Copyright © 1994 by Rita Gilbert. Reprinted with the permission of McGraw-Hill, Inc.

After Reading

A. Vocabulary Check. Look back at the passage to find the answers to these questions. Don't use a dictionary. Numbers in parentheses refer to lines.

1. These two words are frequently used in art history classes. What do they mean?

   • genre (5–10): _____

   • illuminate (15–20): _____

2. The pictures, together with the paragraphs, will help you understand something about these words. What can you guess about them?

   • charming (5–10 and 10–15): _____

   • hut (20–25): _____

   • landscape (20–25): _____

   • cloak (20–25): _____

   • chopping (20–25): _____

   • delightful (30–35): _____

B. Word Journal.   Go back to the passage. Which words are important for you to remember? Put them in your Word Journal.

C. Pronoun Reference.   What does the pronoun mean in each context that follows? Write the meaning on the line.

1. When children start to draw and paint, <u>they</u> deal with the images that <u>they</u> know best.

   they = _____

2. The Limbourg Brothers illuminated one of the most famous books in the history of art, *Les Très Riches Heures.* <u>It</u> contains a calendar.

   it = _____

3. The "February" page depicts a small hut with three people around a fire. <u>They</u> have pulled their clothes back to get maximum warmth from the fire.

   they = _____

4. In Renoir's *Le Moulin de la Galette,* young couples meet at an outdoor cafe, <u>they</u> dance, they fall in love.

   they = _____

5. Segal set up three of his life-size figures in a New York City bus terminal, as if <u>they</u> were waiting in line to buy a ticket.

   they = _____

D. Understanding Italics.   Find the words in the passage that are in italics. What is the reason for the italics? Discuss your answer with a partner.

E. Vocabulary Expansion: A Game!   Work in small groups. Go back to the passage and quickly find as many adjectives as you can. Put them into these categories, if possible. If you're not sure about the category for some adjectives, put them in the box below the chart and discuss them later with the whole class. The group that finds the most adjectives wins the game.

1. Opinion

_____

_____

_____

_____

_____

2. Size

_____

_____

_____

_____

_____

3. Condition

_____

_____

_____

_____

_____

4. Age

_____

_____

_____

_____

_____

5. Color

_____

_____

_____

_____

_____

6. Nationality

_____

_____

_____

_____

_____

Not Sure about the Category		
_____	_____	_____
_____	_____	_____
_____	_____	_____
_____	_____	_____

F. Discussion. In small groups, answer these questions.

1. Which of the genre paintings in the passage do you like most? Why?

2. What are some subjects of genre art in *your* culture? What are people doing in this art? From what period is this art (ancient, eighteenth century, modern, etc.)?

. : : : : Part Four The Mechanics of Writing

In Part Five, you are going to write a comparison-contrast paragraph about two paintings. In your paragraph, you may need to use adjectives, appositives, adjective clauses, participial phrases, prepositional phrases, and transitional expressions of comparison and contrast. Part Four will prepare you for this.

Appositives

An appositive is a noun or noun phrase that comes after another noun or noun phrase. It either means the same as the first noun or gives more information about it. An appositive comes between commas, or it comes after a comma.

Examples: Dr. Chen, <u>our art history professor</u>, has written several textbooks.

The king of Israel, <u>King Josiah</u>, ordered the destruction of all pagan cultures.

She picked up the strange little figure, <u>an ancient perfume bottle</u>.

A. Sentence Combining: Appositives.   Combine the following pairs of sentences. Make the second sentence in each pair into an appositive and add it to the first.

1. This is a statue of Aphrodite.

   Aphrodite was the goddess of love and beauty.

   _____

   _____

2. A thirteenth-century Italian master painted *Madonna Enthroned.*

   A thirteenth-century Italian master was Cimabue.

   _____

   _____

3. The Buddha's hand position symbolizes the giving of gifts.

   The Buddha's hand position is a *mudra.*

   _____

   _____

4. The Virgin Mary is the central figure.

The Virgin Mary is the mother of Christ.

_____

_____

5. The statue was created by one of the finest Greek sculptors.

One of the finest Greek sculptors was Praxiteles.

_____

_____

Adjective Clauses

In Chapter One (page 26) you saw that adjective clauses modify nouns. If the adjective clause adds extra information to a sentence, there are commas around it—or a comma before it and a period after it.

Examples: Renoir, <u>who was a French Impressionist painter,</u> is very popular today.

The painting depicts a Maya ball game, <u>which was very different from ball games these days</u>.

Note: Do not begin an adjective clause with _that_ if there is a comma before it.

B. Sentence Combining: Adjective Clauses.   Combine these pairs of sentences. Make the second sentence in each pair into an adjective clause and add it to the first. Use a comma (or commas).

1. He took a class in art history.

Art history is a required course.

_____

_____

2. This figure is actually a perfume bottle.

This figure looks like a doll.

_____

_____

3. The painting is a memorial to Marilyn Monroe.

Marilyn Monroe was an American actress.

_____

_____

4. Impressionist artists are now favorites among museum goers.

Impressionist artists' work was not appreciated at the time it was created.

_____

_____

5. The Buddha is surrounded by *bodhisattvas.*

Bodhisattvas help other people reach Nirvana.

_____

_____

6. This is a statue of Aphrodite.

Aphrodite was the goddess of love and beauty to the ancient Greeks.

_____

_____

Participial Phrases

A participial phrase, like an appositive or adjective clause, gives information about a noun. One type of participial phrase is a reduced adjective clause.

Examples: The painting has a large central figure <u>that is facing front</u>. =
(adjective clause)

The painting has a large central figure <u>facing front</u>.
(present participial phrase)

The painting <u>that is shown on this page</u> is by Renoir. =
(adjective clause)

The painting <u>shown on this page</u> is by Renoir.
(past participial phrase)

Present participial phrases begin with a present participle (*-ing*). They are in the active voice. Past participial phrases begin with a part participle (*-ed* for regular verbs). They are in the passive voice.

C. Practice.   For each sentence that follows, underline the adjective clause and draw an arrow to the noun that it modifies. Then change the adjective clause to a participial phrase by crossing out the unnecessary words and commas.

1. The central figure is surrounded by smaller figures who are wearing halos.

2. Two artists who were unknown to each other created similar works of art.

3. The anthropomorphic figure that is holding a small bowl is an incense burner.

4. The central figure, who is surrounded by angels, is the Virgin Mary.

5. She is gesturing toward the child who is sitting on her lap.

6. The people who are working in the fields are peasants from the nearby village.

7. *October,* which was painted 150 years before *The Harvesters,* probably influenced Pieter Bruegel.

8. Impressionist artists, who were unappreciated in their lifetime, are favorites among museum goers today.

Prepositional Phrases

These prepositional phrases may be useful when you describe a picture.

the woman arguing w/ her son in the foreground has brought a picnic.

the woman walking with a basket is watching the balloon escape.

in the upper left-hand corner

at the top

in the upper right-hand corner

in the background

in the middle (of the page/ picture)

in the foreground

in the lower left-hand corner

at the bottom

in the lower right-hand corner

In addition, you may need other phrases to explain *which figure* you're discussing in a painting.

Examples: A woman <u>in a hat</u> is in the foreground.
(= a woman *who is wearing a hat*)

A child <u>with a sad expression</u> is next to her.
(= a child *who has a sad expression*)

A woman <u>with a basket of flowers</u> is in the middle.
(= a woman *who has a basket of flowers*)

D. Practice.   Use prepositional phrases to answer these questions about the painting "February," from *Les Très Riches Heures du Duc de Berry.* (See page 85.)

1. Where is the calendar? _____

2. Where is a single tree? _____

3. Where are three women? _____

4. Where are some birds? _____

5. Where is the church? _____

6. Where is the forest? _____

Adjectives: Basic Rules

Adjectives are important when you describe art. An adjective comes before a noun.

Examples: It's a <u>flat</u> painting.

These are <u>realistic</u>* figures.

It's a <u>dramatic</u> scene.

* Note: Adjectives in English are never plural.

An adjective can also come after a verb such as *be, seem,* or *look* (= seem).

Examples: The people look <u>wealthy</u>.

The painting is <u>mysterious</u>.

Participles are often used as adjectives. A present participle (*-ing*) expresses a *cause.* A past participle (*-ed*) expresses a *result* or *effect.*

Examples: This is a <u>charming</u> little figure.

Everyone is <u>charmed</u> by it.

People in 1905 thought it was a <u>shocking</u> painting, but nobody is <u>shocked</u> anymore.

E. Brainstorming. Look at the pictures in Parts One and Two of this chapter. In small groups, think of as many adjectives as possible to describe these pictures and put them into the categories below. If you aren't sure about a category, put the word *somewhere* but put a question mark after it.

1. Opinion	2. Size	3. Condition
_____	_____	_____
_____	_____	_____
_____	_____	_____
_____	_____	_____

4. Age	5. Color	6. Nationality
_____	_____	_____
_____	_____	_____
_____	_____	_____
_____	_____	_____

Order of Adjectives

Sometimes you will use two adjectives to modify a noun. If so, the usual order of those adjectives follows the same order that you see in Exercise E (Brainstorming).

Examples: INCORRECT: This is a <u>little charming</u> figure.

CORRECT: This is a <u>charming little</u> figure.
            (opinion) (size)

INCORRECT: It's an <u>Edomite ancient</u> figure.

CORRECT: It's an <u>ancient Edomite</u> figure.
            (age) (nationality)

Occasionally, you will need to use three adjectives. If so, follow this same order.

Example: This is a <u>charming little Edomite</u> figure.
            (opinion) (size) (nationality)

F. Practice.   Add these adjectives to the sentences.

1. It's a statue. (Italian/huge)

_____

2. There is a house in the foreground. (large/unpainted)

_____

3. This is a painting. (modern/strange/American)

_____

4. These are rooms. (dark/small/uncomfortable)

_____

5. It's a scene. (Chinese/little/pleasant)

_____

6. In the foreground there is a dog. (black/tired/old)

_____

Transitional Expressions: Comparison-Contrast

In Chapter Two you learned many transitional expressions. Here are some more.

similarly in a similar way both . . . and	Use these to express how two items are similar.
in contrast while	Use these to express how two items are different.

Follow the rules for adverbial conjunctions (page 56) for *similarly, in a similar way,* and *in contrast.*

Examples: In the Tibetan painting, the Buddha is surrounded by smaller figures wearing halos. <u>Similarly</u>, in the Italian painting, Mary is surrounded by angels with halos.

Picasso's early paintings were realistic; <u>in contrast</u>, his later work is completely abstract.

Use this structure for *both . . . and:*

> both + NOUN (or NOUN PHRASE) + and + NOUN (or NOUN PHRASE)

Example: <u>Both</u> the Buddha <u>and</u> Mary are* surrounded by smaller figures.

Use *while* (= *although* or *but*) between two independent clauses. (See Appendix 3.)

Example: Picasso's early work is realistic, <u>while</u> his later work is abstract.

* Note: Use a plural verb.

G. Sentence Combining: Expressions of Comparison-Contrast.   Combine the following pairs of sentences. Choose a logical transitional expression for each.

1. The central figure of the Buddha isn't holding anything.

The Virgin Mary is holding the baby Jesus.

_____

_____

2. *Tathagata Buddha* is a religious painting.

Madonna Enthroned is a religious painting.

_____

_____

3. *Tathagata Buddha* was created for Buddhists in Tibet.

Madonna Enthroned was created for Christian Italians.

_____

_____

4. The Buddha has a serene expression.

The Virgin Mary has a serene expression.

_____

_____

5. *Bodhisattvas* are beings who help people to reach Nirvana.

Angels help people to reach heaven.

_____

_____

Part Five Writing in the Academic World

Before Writing

A. Choosing a Topic.   You're going to write a paragraph of comparison-contrast about two paintings. It's important to choose a pair of paintings that you feel comfortable with. Also, you need to have enough—but not *too* much—to say about these paintings. Look over the following pairs of paintings. Choose one pair that you would like to write about. (You can change your mind later if you want.)

1a.

Lamentation, from Avignon, France. 1320–1350

1b.

The Death of General Wolfe, by Benjamin West (American). 1770

2a.

Peasant Family, by Louis le Nain (French). About 1640

2b.

Madame Charpentier and her Children, by Renoir (French). 1878

3a.

The Harvesters, by Pieter Bruegal the Elder (Dutch). 1565

3b.

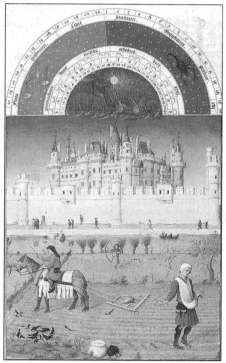

October, from *Les Tres Riches Heures*, by the Limbourg Brothers (French). 1413–1416

4a.

Cooling Off by the Riverbank, by Kitagawa
Utamaro (Japanese). Late 18th century

4b.

In the Omnibus, by Mary Cassatt
(American). 1891

B. Brainstorming: Using Adjectives.
Copy the title of each picture (1a–4b) on a piece of paper. Leave a lot of space under each one. In small groups, think of as many adjectives as possible for each picture. Write these adjectives under the title of each picture. This is a good opportunity to learn new words from other students in your group, to ask your teacher for help with some words, and to use a dictionary (if necessary).

C. Writing Strategy Review: Identifying a Good Topic Sentence.
Circle the letter of the better topic sentence in each pair. Then circle the topic of that sentence and underline the controlling idea.

1a. The theme of both *Lamentation* and *The Death of General Wolfe* is the death of a leader, but the two paintings differ greatly in the details and in style.

b. *Lamentation* and *The Death of General Wolfe* are both about death.

2a. Louis le Nain's *Peasant Family* and Renoir's *Madame Charpentier and her Children* are beautiful portraits.

b. Both Louis le Nain's *Peasant Family* and Renoir's *Madame Charpentier and her Children* are French family portraits, but for the most part, the similarity ends there.

3a. Pieter Bruegal surely owes a debt to his predecessors, the Limbourg Brothers, for while *The Harvesters* differs from *October* in composition and style, the subject is the same—peasants working in the fields.

b. In *October,* peasants are planting seeds in a field while in *The Harvesters,* painted 150 years later, some peasants are harvesting wheat from a field, and others are resting in the shade of a tree.

4a. Mary Cassatt's *In the Omnibus* clearly shows the influence of Japanese woodblock prints in general and perhaps Kitagawa Utamaro's *Cooling Off by the Riverbank* in particular.

b. Kitagawa Utamaro's *Cooling Off by the Riverbank* and Mary Cassatt's *In the Omnibus* both depict two women and a child.

5a. *Tathagata Buddha* and *Madonna Enthroned* are two very interesting religious paintings from the thirteenth century.

b. *Tathagata Buddha* and *Madonna Enthroned* are quite different in content, but they are surprisingly similar in form.

D. Gathering Supporting Material.   After you choose your topic, you need to decide what to say about it. This chart will help you to study the elements of the pair of paintings that you have chosen. Fill in the chart with words and phrases; do not use complete sentences. (You might want to work with another student.)

Elements	Painting 1: Title: _____	Painting 2: Title: _____
subject (theme)		
details		
period (time)		
culture/country		
artist (if known)		
emotional qualities (dark? charming? dramatic? etc.)		
style (realistic? stylized? etc.)		
space (flat or deep)		
other points (design, etc.)		

E. Organizing Supporting Material. Use the information from your chart to help you find similarities and differences between the two paintings. (You don't have to include *every* element, however.) Write only notes; don't write complete sentences.

<table>
<tr><td align="center">**Similarities**</td><td align="center">**Differences**</td></tr>
</table>

_____   _____

_____   _____

_____   _____

_____   _____

_____   _____

_____   _____

_____   _____

Writing

writing Strategy

Writing a Paragraph of Comparison-Contrast

In a paragraph of comparison-contrast, you *compare* two items (tell how they are similar) and *contrast* them (tell how they are different). Both items must be in the same class; in other words, they have to be related to each other in some way. You can compare and contrast two houses or two animals or two economic systems or two paintings, for example. However, you cannot compare or contrast a house and an animal because they don't belong to the same group (class). After you choose two items to compare and contrast, you must have *at least* one similarity and one difference. In your paragraph, you need to give equal weight to each point; that is, don't spend most of the paragraph telling about just one point.

One way to organize information in a comparison-contrast paragraph is with an **alternating pattern.** In this pattern, after the topic sentence, present each point (for example, *subject, period, artist*) and discuss the similarities or differences. Group the similarities together and the differences together.

Example: Plan for a paragraph about two paintings:

Tathagata Buddha	*Madonna Enthroned*	
√ religion—Buddhist	√ religion—Christianity	Differences
√ holding nothing	√ holding the baby Jesus	
√ wearing very little	√ wearing long robes	

√ period: thirteenth century
√ large central figure facing front
√ emotional qualities: calm, serene
√ details: symbolic hand gesture
central figure surrounded by figures with halos
small figures with halos help people
} Similarities

After you have organized the similarities and differences in this way, you can expand your phrases into sentences and write your paragraph.

Example: Two religious paintings, *Tathagata Buddha* from Tibet and Cimabue's *Madonna Enthroned* from Florence, were created four thousand miles apart and for different religions, so they are quite different in content; nevertheless, they are surprisingly similar in form. *Tathagata Buddha* is, of course, a Buddhist painting, and *Madonna Enthroned* is Christian. The Buddha, the central figure in *Tathagata Buddha,* isn't holding anything; in contrast, the Virgin Mary, the central figure in *Madonna Enthroned,* is holding the baby Jesus. The Buddha is wearing very little clothing but elaborate jewelry while the Virgin is wearing long robes. However, these paintings have more similarities than differences. Both were created in the thirteenth century and have a large central figure facing front. The central figure in each painting has a calm, serene expression and a symbolic hand gesture; the Buddha's hand position symbolizes the giving of gifts while Mary gestures toward her son, symbolic of the hope of the world. Finally, both

topic sentence

differences

similarities

the Buddha and the Virgin Mary are surrounded by smaller figures wearing halos. In *Tathagata Buddha*, these smaller figures, *bodhisattvas*, help people to reach Nirvana. Similarly, the angels surrounding the Virgin Mary help people to reach heaven. Clearly, two artists unknown to each other created quite similar paintings for their different religions.

conclusion

Notice in the example:

* the use of expressions for comparison and contrast:

  both . . . and
  similarly
  in contrast
  while

* the use of appositives

* the alternating pattern

* the fact that differences are given first and similarities next.*

* Note: You might decide to give the similarities first. It depends on your material.

Writing Assignment: First Draft.   Use your notes on similarities and differences from page 103 as a guide. (You might not want to include *all* of this information.) Decide how to group the similarities and differences. Then write your paragraph of comparison-contrast. Be sure to

√ have a topic sentence (one from page 101 or your own)

√ have a clear alternating pattern

√ have a concluding sentence.

After Writing

A. Self-Check.   Read over your paragraph. Answer the questions on the following checklist. Write yes or no.

B. Classmate's Check.   Exchange papers with a classmate. Check each other's paragraphs. Write yes or no on your classmate's checklist.

editing Checklist

Points To Check For	My Check	My Classmate's Check
1. Is the paragraph form correct (indentation, margins)?		
2. Is there a topic sentence that includes the main topic and a controlling idea?		
3. Is there at least one similarity between the two paintings?		
4. Is there at least one difference between the two paintings?		
5. Is there a clear alternating pattern?		
6. Is there correct use of transition words?		
7. Is there a concluding sentence?		
8. Other: _____		

Second Draft.   Use the answers on the checklist to help you to rewrite your paragraph. Then give your paragraph to your teacher.

About the five pieces of art on pages 74–76 in Part One:

1. This is a piece of *netsuke* from Japan. When people wore kimonos, the *netsuke* was attached to a short rope. On the other end of the rope was an *inro,* which held small items that the person wanted to carry, much as we might carry a wallet or small purse today.
2. This is called *Marilyn.* There is a photo of Marilyn Monroe and also a number of symbolic images associated with her.
3. This is an *akua'ba* figure from the Ashanti people of Ghana.
4. This is a perfume flask (container) from an area near the Dead Sea.
5. This is a painting of Mayan ball players. The Maya lived in Yucatan, southern Mexico, and Central America. Their ball games were not for entertainment, as ours are today. Instead, the ball game was a religious ritual. The winning team had to get a heavy ball through a small circular opening in a high stone carving. The leader of the winning team was sacrificed to the gods.

chapter Four

The Ancient World: Egypt

In this chapter, you'll read about ancient Egyptian history and art. You'll also apply the "rules" of Egyptian art to describe, analyze, and write about one piece of ancient art.

⁘ **Part One** Rules of Egyptian Art

Before Reading

Discussion.   Look at the following wall painting. In small groups, examine the details of the painting and answer these questions.

1. Which people are Nakht and his wife? Why do you think so?

2. Who might the other people be?

3. What are the people doing? Describe as many activities as possible.

4. Do these figures look realistic? Why or why not? What seems strange about them?

Nakht and His Wife. Copy of a wall painting from the tomb of Nakht, c. 1425 BC, Thebes, Egypt.
The Metropolitan Museum of Art, New York

Reading

As you read the following passage, think about the answer to this question.

• Why did the style of Egyptian art stay almost the same for 3,000 years?

The Rules of Egyptian Art

Just for a few moments, imagine some famous paintings of one or two hundred years ago. Can you picture these in your mind? Now imagine the most modern abstract art of today. In only one to two hundred years, there have been huge changes in the form and content of art. In contrast, the char-
5 acteristics of ancient Egyptian art remained nearly the same for almost three *thousand* years.

Many characteristics of Egyptian art can already be seen in the famous *Palette of King Narmer,*
10 which was created in about 3100 BC, during the Old Kingdom. The palette, probably used for mixing cosmetics, depicts King Narmer holding an enemy by the hair.
15 Narmer's size and central position indicate his high status. The design is neat and carefully organized. The palette is divided by horizontal lines into sections. We
20 see two fallen enemies in the lowest section. In the central section, a servant holds Narmer's sandals, which indicates that Narmer is probably standing in a
25 temple or on holy ground. The bird in the upper right hand corner is a falcon—Horus, the god of Upper Egypt. The palette is filled with images but, somehow,
30 doesn't seem crowded. We can clearly see the details. Even so, there is something flat and a little strange about these images.

Why did this flat style remain constant for thousands of years? It wasn't
35 due to a lack of ability. Egyptian artists were certainly *able* to create full, natural
images. We know this from the lovely, realistic animals in many of their wall
paintings. [See page 108.] And, of course, there is the famous portrait of Queen
Nefertiti, which seems real enough to come alive and speak to us. Nevertheless,
the flat artistic style remained the same in most Egyptian art because the artists
40 were following a strict set of rules written by powerful priests. These rules
might look like this:

Queen Nefertiti

Rules for Artists

1. The pharaoh (king) or most important person must be the largest. Servants, children, and unimportant wives must be smaller.
2. Men have dark or red skin. Women have light or yellow skin. (It doesn't matter what their real skin color is.)
3. People of high status—especially the pharaoh—must look stiff and serious. They should appear frozen and unmoving.
4. People of low status may be shown in more natural positions as they hunt, fish, plant or harvest crops, and do other work.
5. Depict animals as naturally as possible in correct biological details.
6. Don't leave empty areas. Fill the space with human figures, animals, plants, or hieroglyphics (writing).
7. When you create a human image (especially an important person), be sure to show all parts of the body from the most familiar point of view:
   • The head, arms, and feet must be seen from the side.
   • The shoulders and eye must be seen from the front.
   A complete, clear image is necessary. If an arm, for example, is hidden behind the body, the person's *ka* (spirit) will live forever without an arm.
8. In the tomb of a dead pharaoh or important person, paint his wife, servants, and slaves. They will be with him and take care of him for all eternity—forever.

Sources: "Rules of Egyptian Art" adapted, in part, from Rita Gilbert, *Living With Art,* Fourth Edition, pp. 353–355. Copyright © 1994 by Rita Gilbert. Reprinted with the permission of McGraw-Hill, Inc. "Rules of Egyptian Art" adapted, in part, from Gene A. Mitler, *Art in Focus,* pp. 153–154, Copyright © 1994 by Glencoe/McGraw-Hill. Reprinted with the permission of the publishers.

After Reading

A. Main Ideas.   Go back to the reading. When you find the answers to these questions, mark them with a felt-tip pen.

1. If Egyptian art didn't change much for 3,000 years, was there a problem with the ability of the artists?

2. Why didn't Egyptian art change much for a such a long time?

B. Application.   Look back at the wall painting of *Nakht and His Wife*. Fill in the chart with examples from this painting. Then add the number of the rule (from Rules for Artists) that told the artist what to do.

Elements	Examples from the Wall Painting from the Tomb of Nakht	Rule #
space		
animals		
people: color		
size		
activity		
style		
actions of people (besides Nakht)		

C. Response Writing.   For ten minutes, write as much as you can about the wall painting *Nakht and His Wife*. Describe it and explain in your own words why the artist used these elements.

. : : : : : **Part Two** Finds Reveal Much of Life at Pyramids

Before Reading

A. Making Predictions.   Most people know that the pyramids of ancient Egypt were tombs for the dead pharaohs. However, until recently, we didn't know much about the people who built the pyramids. With a partner, answer these questions.

Egyptian pyramids at Giza—tombs of the pharaohs, built c. 2550 BC

1. In your opinion, who built the pyramids? What was the status of these builders?

2. What might their lives have been like? How were their lives different from the pharaohs' lives?

B. Vocabulary Preparation.   The following newspaper article has some words that will be new to you. What can you guess about each underlined word that follows? Write your guess on each line and compare your answers with another student's.

1. The builders of the pyramids lived in a village not far from their worksite. When they died, their families buried them in tombs in a nearby <u>cemetery</u>.

   My Guess: _____

2. That town is built on the side of a mountain. Houses up at the top of the <u>cliff</u> are the most expensive because they have a beautiful view. Houses down at the bottom of the <u>slope</u> are cheap because there is no view. (Note: In this context, <u>cliff</u> and <u>slope</u> have the same meaning.)

   My Guess: _____

3. Art historians and archaeologists are excited about the new discoveries. Every day, diggers at the <u>excavations</u> find another ancient perfume jar or cooking pot. Sometimes they find a complete tomb.

   My Guess: _____

reading Strategy

Guessing Meaning from Context

Sometimes you can guess the meaning of a new word if its *opposite* is in the context.

Example: Houses down at the bottom of the cliff were undesirable and unwanted because of
the bad location, but houses up at the top of the cliff were <u>sought after</u>.

Here we see that <u>sought after</u> means the opposite of "undesirable" or "unwanted." Therefore, <u>sought
after</u> means "desirable" or "wanted."

4. The pharaohs often had more than one wife, but most ordinary Egyptians were <u>monogamous</u>.

My Guess: _____

5. His moustache wasn't large or messy. It was <u>neatly trimmed</u> and as thin as a pencil.

My Guess: _____

6. Most of the people who built the houses were workers with no special ability; however, a few
were <u>artisans</u>—<u>skilled workers</u>. (Note: In this context, <u>artisans</u> and <u>skilled workers</u> have the
same meaning.)

My Guess: _____

C. Parts of Speech.   Identify the part of speech of each underlined word that follows. Then write
your guess about the meaning.

1. I don't know why people just <u>dump</u> their garbage here!

Part of Speech: _____

My Guess: _____

2. These days, there are huge garbage <u>dumps</u> outside most big cities. In ancient times, of course, there were garbage dumps, too. Modern archaeologists can learn a lot about people from the things that they threw away.

Part of Speech: _____

My Guess: _____

3. Zahi Hawass is an Egyptologist who studies ancient life in the area of the pyramids in Giza. Every year he <u>finds</u> more information about the people who built the pyramids.

Part of Speech: _____

My Guess: _____

4. There are some exciting new <u>finds</u> in Egypt.

Part of Speech: _____

My Guess: _____

5. A mystery <u>remains</u>: How did the pyramid builders move the huge stones?

Part of Speech: _____

My Guess: _____

6. We had a wonderful dinner party, but after the guests left, we had to clean up the <u>remains</u>.

Part of Speech: _____

My Guess: _____

Reading

As you read the newspaper article, mark with a felt-tip pen anything that surprises you or is interesting about life in ancient Egypt.

Finds reveal much of life at pyramids

■ **Old clues:**
Cemetery dig gives new look at ancient Egypt workers.

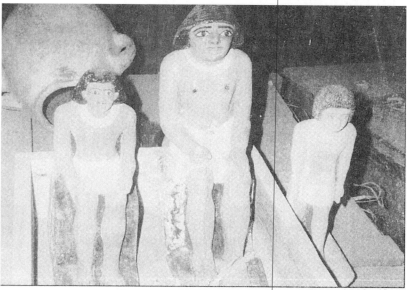

Associated Press

Three statues found recently in a Giza Plateau cemetery show ages in the life of one man, a blue-collar worker from 4,600 years ago named She-dou.

GIZA PLATEAU, Egypt (AP)—Beer in the morning, beer in the afternoon, beer at night. A little wine thrown in for good measure. And after a hard day of cutting stones for the pharaoh, time and energy left for a bit of hanky-panky.

Life wasn't all work and no play for the workers who built the pyramids, tombs and temples of Giza Plateau.

"History is life," said Egyptologist Zahi Hawass, in charge of an ancient cemetery yielding volumes of information about the life and times of the pyramid work force.

Archaeologists poking through garbage dumps, examining skeletons, probing texts and studying remains of beer jars, wine vats and bakeries have discovered all kinds of information about the pyramid builders:

■ Beer was dished out three times daily. There were five kinds of beer and four kinds of wine available.

■ They could build strong bodies in 12 ways—with 12 varieties of bread.

■ Neatly trimmed pencil moustaches were in vogue, and workers had nicknames still popular today, like Didi and Mimi.

■ Their lives averaged 36 to 38 years, and industrial accidents took a toll. Six skeletons revealed deaths from injuries. Many others had bent spines

from the weight of stone blocks they carried.

■ Ordinary Egyptians were monogamous, but some played around. And they kept up with the Joneses.

Much of the new information comes from excavations over the past nine months in cemeteries found near the pyramids about three years ago.

Recently found texts show that the pyramid builders were not slaves, as was long believed, but were free Egyptians working for the gods. The pharaoh provided them with food, clothing and shelter.

"Everything about this cemetery disputes the idea that these people were slaves," Hawass said last week.

It is not clear how many workers were involved in building them, but the three major pyramids at Giza and the queen's pyramids near-by

were built over a 70-year period beginning about 2,551 B.C., when Cheops ascended to the throne.

Skilled workers, probably sought-after artisans, were buried in 43 tombs lined up at the top of the cliffside cemetery. They were the prime burial sites, affording views of the pyramids a few miles across the dunes.

Foremen were buried in smaller tombs just down the slope. At the bottom were workers, often buried only in deep shafts.

Archaeologists have found 600 tombs of foremen and workers. Job descriptions include "decorator of tombs," "the official in charge of one side of the pyramid," or "overseer of the stone movers."

The most important tomb found so far belonged to She-dou, a blue-collar worker

identified as a servant of the goddess of war and hunting, Neith.

In a secret compartment to the rear archaeologists found four painted statues of She-dou. The largest, measuring 29 inches, represents She-dou in a short white kilt, his neck ringed by a wide collar adorned with blue, white and yellow stones.

A neighboring tomb gave excavators another surprise. It was already known that, unlike the pharaohs, ordinary Egyptians were monogamous. But the man buried in this tomb lay between his wife and another woman.

"Texts show she had to be a girlfriend," said Hawass. "It's surprising the wife put up with it."

The upper classes avoided such scandal because they were in the public eye.

Source: "Finds Reveal Much of Life at Pyramids" from *The Star Free Press* (May 31, 1993). Associated Press story. Reprinted with the permission of the Associated Press.

After Reading

A. Main Idea.   Which one-sentence paragraph gives the main idea of the article?

 reading Strategy

Understanding Idioms

An idiom is a phrase that has a different meaning from the meaning of each separate word. Idioms are often fun to learn, but they can also be difficult in a new language. Sometimes you can guess the meaning from the context.

Example: I bought only three pounds of apples at the farmers' market, but the seller was really nice and threw in a few free apples <u>for good measure</u>.

   (<u>For good measure</u> probably means "in addition" or "as something more or extra.")

B. Practice.   There are several idioms in the article. What do you think they mean? With a partner, discuss the possible meanings.

1. He worked very hard all his life and didn't often relax. He smoked a lot, ate junk food, and worried all the time. Unfortunately, this lifestyle <u>took a toll</u> on his health.

2. Social status and wealth are important to him and his wife. They try hard to <u>keep up with the Joneses</u>: they wear stylish clothes, have hairstyles that are <u>in vogue</u>, have new cars, and buy fashionable furniture. However, it's hard for them to pay for all of this because they're both <u>blue-collar workers</u>.

3. I think he has a girlfriend. Of course, his wife doesn't know that he's <u>playing around</u>. If she knew, she would never <u>put up with this hanky-panky</u> of his. She would tell him to leave his girlfriend or to get out.

C. Word Journal.   Go back to the article. Which words or idioms are important for you to remember? Put them in your Word Journal.

D. Recognizing Tone.   In your opinion, what is the tone—that is, the general quality—of the article? Circle the number of one answer. Why did you choose this answer?

1. The article is very serious and academic.

2. The article is just fun and doesn't give any important information.

3. The article is light (not very serious) in tone but is also informative on an academic subject.

E. Identifying Causes and Effects.

E. Identifying Causes and Effects. Finish each sentence on the left (the effect or result) with a logical item from the right (the cause or reason). Write a letter on each line.

Effects

1. Workers had bent spines because they _____.

2. Some workers were buried in tombs at the top of the cliffside because they _____.

3. Some workers were buried at the bottom of the cliffside cemetery because they _____.

4. Workers died quite young; their lives averaged only 36 to 38 years because they _____.

5. The upper classes avoided "playing around" and other "hanky-panky" because they _____.

Causes

a. had higher status than others.

b. suffered accidents and injuries.

c. were in the public eye.

d. carried heavy stone blocks.

e. had lower status than others.

F. Making Inferences.

F. Making Inferences. These three inferences can be made from the article. Find specific information to support each inference.

1. Inference: Life for the builders of the pyramids wasn't all bad.

   Support: _____

2. Inference: Life was physically hard on the workers.

   Support: _____

3. Inference: There were three classes of pyramid workers.

   Support: _____

G. Discussion.

G. Discussion. In small groups, discuss this question: What in the article surprised or interested you about life in ancient Egypt?

. . : : ∶ ∶ **Part Three** Reading in the Academic World

Before Reading

A. Vocabulary Preparation.

The following textbook passage has some words that will be new to you. You can understand something about many of them from the context. What can you guess about each underlined word that follows? Write your guess for each of these words. Then compare your answers with another student's.

1. There was a <u>succession</u> of wars—one after another after another.

   My Guess: _____

2. The <u>ruler</u> who sat on the throne of Egypt was not always a great leader, but in the eyes of his people, he was both pharaoh and god.

   My Guess: _____

3. King Tutankhamen's tomb was filled with <u>magnificent</u> art—gold and silver, paintings, statues, and beautiful furniture.

   My Guess: _____

4. After 4,000 years, the wall painting was in poor condition, but art experts at the museum were able to <u>restore</u> it. Now it looks almost exactly as it looked when it was new.

   My Guess: _____

5. They made the <u>journey</u> from Memphis to the new capital, Thebes. When they finally arrived, they were hot and tired.

   My Guess: _____

6. He walked <u>aimlessly</u> through the old city. He had no purpose, no idea of where to go or what to do.

   My Guess: _____

7. Ancient Egyptians <u>went to great lengths</u> to protect the body of the pharaoh. They were prepared to do anything necessary to keep his body safe.

   My Guess: _____

B. Thinking Ahead.

Before you read, briefly review the Rules for Artists (page 110). Then look over the pictures in the textbook passage (pages 119–121). Do all of these pictures appear to follow the rules?

Reading

As you read the textbook passage, think about the answer to this question

• How was art a mirror for the three periods in ancient Egyptian history?

Egyptian Civilization: A Brief History

It is usual to divide the long history of Egypt into three periods: the Old Kingdom, the Middle Kingdom, and the New Kingdom. These are further divided into dynasties. A dynasty was a period when a single family provided a succession of rulers. When one pharaoh died, a successor was chosen from the same family. It was important to keep the blood of a royal family pure; therefore, the pharaoh was not allowed to marry outside of the immediate family.

The Old Kingdom

The earliest dynastic period began around 3100 BC when Upper and Lower Egypt were united by a powerful pharaoh named Menes. Menes established his capital at Memphis and founded the first of the thirty-one Egyptian dynasties.

It was during the Old Kingdom that the pyramids were built. These massive tombs were an attempt to keep the body of the pharaoh safe. The Egyptians believed that the soul, or *ka*, remained with the body until death. At death, the ka left the body for a time, but it later returned and united with the body again for the journey to the next world. If the body was destroyed, the ka had to travel aimlessly for all eternity. For this reason, the Egyptians went to great lengths to protect the body—especially the body of the pharaoh, for he was both a king and, in the eyes of the people, a god.

Often, however, thieves broke into the pyramids. They stole the gold and other treasures and destroyed the pharaoh's body. Consequently, sculptors began to create statues of the pharaoh, such as the portrait of Khafre on this throne. They put these statues inside the tomb so that the ka could enter this stone statue for the journey to the next world.

Khafre, c. 2600 BC, Egyptian Museum, Cairo, Egypt

The Middle Kingdom

The Middle Kingdom was a time of law and order in Egypt until foreign armies attacked Egypt for the first time, around 1800 BC. The Hyksos from western Asia had horses and
45 chariots. They easily won battles because the Egyptians were fighting on foot. The Hyksos remained in Egypt for two hundred years. When the Egyptians finally learned how to use horses and chariots, they forced the
50 Hyksos to leave their country.

During the Middle Kingdom, Egyptians stopped building pyramids and began to build pharaohs' tombs in rock cliffs, instead. Much of the sculpture was destroyed by the
55 Hyksos. Perhaps one incomplete portrait of King Sesostris III, which was created during this difficult period, represents the time. This portrait is very different from Old Kingdom portraits of rulers. It is a surprisingly
60 realistic face. The firmly set mouth and lines above the eyes express deep worry and a troubled emotional condition.

Portrait of Sesostris III, c. 1850 BC (Middle Kingdom)

The New Kingdom

The third period of Egyptian history, the New Kingdom, began in 1570 BC. With a
65 knowledge of horses and chariots, Egypt became a military power and ruled over neighboring nations. Thebes, the royal capital, became the most magnificent city in the world. It was a Golden Age of Egypt.

70 One pharaoh in 1372 BC broke with Egyptian tradition for a short time. When Amenhotep IV came to power, he moved the capital, changed his name to Ikhnaton, and established a monotheistic religion, with
75 Aton (symbolized as the sun) as the one god. This was an attempt to break the enormous power of the priests of other gods. However, after Ikhnaton's death this new religion did not remain. The capital was returned to
80 Thebes, and the old polytheistic faith was restored. But Egypt's time of power and glory was ending. When Alexander the Great of Macedonia brought his army to Egypt in 332 BC, the New Kingdom came to
85 a close.

Ikhnaton influenced not only the religion but also the art of his time. The strict rules for artists became relaxed, and art became less stiff, more realistic. From this
90 period we have the wonderful lifelike portrait of Nefertiti [see page 110], Ikhnaton's wife. And a charming wall painting of his daughters shows them with natural, playful gestures. Most surprisingly, portraits of
95 Ikhnaton himself show him as he really looked—and he was not handsome.

With Ikhnaton's death, the old rules for artists returned. Nevertheless, we can still see some of his influence in much of the art,
100 such as the tomb art of Ikhnaton's famous young successor, Tutankhamen.

Daughters of Ikhnaton (fragment of a mural), detail c. 1365 BC

Ikhnaton, c. 1360 BC

The throne of
Tutankhamen,
Egyptian Museum,
Cairo, Egypt

After Reading

A. Comprehension Check.   With a partner, discuss the answers to these questions.

1. Which period was a difficult time when foreign armies fought in Egypt and art was destroyed?

2. During which period were the pyramids built?

3. During which period did an unusual pharaoh rule Egypt? (He changed the religion, the capital, his name, and the rules for art.) Who was he?

B. Vocabulary Check.   Look back at the passage to find words for these definitions. Numbers in parentheses refer to lines.

1. a period when a single family leads a country (5–10): _____

2. began or set up (two words) (15–20): _____ or _____

3. huge and heavy (15–20): _____

4. very beautiful and valuable things (30–35): _____

5. vehicles from ancient times that horses pulled (45–50): _____

C. Stems and Affixes.   Here are five more word stems. Use them to analyze the words in the sentences that follow. Work with a partner.

Stems	Meaning
capit-	head
gam-	marriage
mono-	one
poly-	many
the-	god

1. The upper classes in Egypt were usually <u>monogamous</u>, except for the pharaohs.

2. Ikhnaton moved the <u>capital</u> of Egypt from Thebes to a place near Tell el 'Amarna.

3. Egyptian religion was <u>polytheistic</u> for thousands of years.

4. One pharaoh changed the religion to <u>monotheism</u> for the short time of his rule.

D. Vocabulary Expansion.

Your vocabulary will grow faster if you learn different parts of speech when you learn a new word. Use the textbook passage and a dictionary to fill in these words.

Verb	Noun	
_____	succession	(situation)
	successor _____	(person)
_____	_____	(situation)
	ruler	(person)
establish	_____	
restore	_____	

E. Word Journal.

Go back to the passage. Which words are important for you to remember? Put them in your Word Journal.

F. Pronoun Reference.

What does the pronoun mean in each context that follows? Write the meaning on the line.

1. At death, the ka left the body for a time, but <u>it</u> later returned and united with the body again.

it = _____

2. Thieves often broke into the pyramids. <u>They</u> stole gold and other treasures.

they = _____

3. Sculptors began to create statues of the pharaoh, such as the portrait of Khafre. <u>They</u> put these statues inside the tomb.

they = _____

4. A charming wall painting of his daughters shows <u>them</u> with natural, playful gestures.

them = _____

G. Identifying Causes and Effects.   Look back at the textbook passage to find answers to these questions. (Hint: Look for the expressions *therefore, for this reason, consequently,* and *because.*)

1. Why was the pharaoh not allowed to marry outside of the immediate family?

_____

_____

2. Why did the Egyptians go to great lengths to protect the body of the pharaoh?

_____

_____

3. Why did sculptors begin to create statues of the pharaohs?

_____

_____

4. Why did the Hyksos easily win battles against the Egyptians?

_____

_____

. : : ! ! **Part Four** The Mechanics of Writing

In Part Five, you are going to write a paragraph about Egyptian art. In your paragraph, you'll need to explain the artist's reasons for the style of a painting. Part Four will help you to write about causes, effects, and purposes.

Infinitives of Purpose

An infinitive (*to* + the simple form of a verb) can answer the question "Why."

Example: Artists depicted the pharaoh as stiff and unmoving <u>to show</u> his high status.

   (<u>to show</u> his high status = because they wanted to show his high status)

A. Practice. Match each sentence on the left with a purpose for it on the right. Then write complete sentences on the lines that follow. Use an infinitive of purpose in each sentence. Follow the example.

1. Mix blue and yellow. (*c*)

2. Mix red and yellow. (   )

3. Use plants, animals, and hieroglyphics. (   )

4. Make the pharaoh larger than other figures. (   )

5. There should be servants in tomb art. (   )

a. Fill empty space.

b. Take care of pharaohs for eternity.

c. Make green.

d. Show his importance.

e. Make orange.

1. ___Mix blue and yellow to make green._____

2. _____

3. _____

4. _____

5. _____

Using Transitional Expressions of Cause and Effect: Subordinating Conjunctions

Subordinating conjunctions are a common type of transitional expression. To express a cause and effect relationship between two sentences, you can join the sentences with one of these words:

because

since ⎫
as   ⎭ = because

Examples: The artist used hieroglyphics <u>because</u> he needed to fill in empty space. (Note: no comma.)

<u>Because</u> the artist needed to fill in empty space, he used hieroglyphics. (Note: comma.)

There is a comma after the first clause if the sentence begins with the subordinating conjunction. There is no comma if the subordinating conjunction is in the middle.

<u>Because</u>, <u>since</u>, or <u>as</u> begins the clause that contains the cause or reason. The other clause (the main clause) expresses the effect or result. <u>Because</u> is more frequently used than <u>since</u> or <u>as</u>.

B. Sentence Combining: Subordinating Conjunctions.   Combine the following pairs of sentences in two ways each. Use subordinating conjunctions. (Note: Before you write, decide which sentence is the cause or reason and which is the result or effect.)

1. Art historians now know more about the lives of the pyramid builders.

Archaeologists have been excavating the workers' tombs.

a. _____

_____

b. _____

_____

2. Many people had thought that the pyramid builders were all slaves.

Many people were surprised. (Note: Use a pronoun.)

a. _____

_____

b. _____

_____

3. Expert opinion is that pyramid builders did not all have the same status.

Pyramid builders had tombs of different quality. (Note: Use a pronoun.)

a. _____

_____

b. _____

_____

4. Skilled artisans with higher status than workers were buried in tombs along the top of the cliff.

Tombs with a view of the pyramids were considered desirable.

a. _____

_____

b. _____

_____

Transitional Expressions and Phrases

If the cause or reason is a noun or noun phrase (instead of a clause), use <u>due to</u> or <u>because of</u>.

Examples: Skilled artisans were buried in tombs of better quality <u>because of</u> their higher status.

(noun phrase)

<u>Because of</u> their higher status, skilled artisans were buried in tombs of better quality.
(noun phrase)

C. Practice.   In the following paragraph, fill in the blanks with <u>because</u>, <u>since</u>, <u>as</u>, <u>because of</u>, or <u>due to</u>. Don't use the same expression more than once.

_____ ancient Egyptian religious beliefs, much of what we know today about the
   1

people comes from their tombs. Great care was taken to protect and preserve the body after death

_____ people believed that a person's *ka,* or soul, needed a body in which to live. It
   2

was especially necessary to preserve the body of the pharaoh _____ he was seen as both
                                                                                3

a king and a god. People believed that he would join the other gods when he died. _____
                                                                                         4

a need to keep his body safe, the Egyptians built the massive, amazing pyramids that we see today.

However, the enormous effort that went into the pyramids was not just for the sake of the pharaoh

himself. The people of ancient Egypt would do almost anything for their king _____
                                                                                    5

he was seen as responsible for order in the universe.

Conjunctions of Cause and Effect: Review

In Chapters One and Two, you saw the rules for coordinating and adverbial conjunctions. (To check these rules, see pages 248–250.) You now know several ways to join the same pair of sentences. This is good to know because in a paragraph that gives many causes or reasons, you don't want to use *because* over and over. You'll want variety in your use of transitional expressions. So far, you have studied three groups of conjunctions for cause and effect:

so (= that's why)
for (= because)

since
as
because

consequently
as a result
for this reason   } = so
therefore

D. Review: Conjunctions of Cause and Effect.   Rewrite each sentence in two different ways, as indicated, keeping the same meaning. Be sure to use correct punctuation. You'll need to change the order of the clauses in some cases. Also, make sure that the subject of the first clause is a noun and the subject of the second clause is a pronoun.

1. Workers had bent spines because they carried heavy stone blocks.

   a. (for) _____

   _____

   b. (therefore) _____

   _____

2. Some workers were buried in tombs at the top of the cliffside cemetery because they had higher status than other workers.

   a. (so) _____

   _____

   b. (for this reason) _____

   _____

3. Some workers were buried at the bottom of the cliffside cemetery because they had lower status than others.

   a. (for) _____

   _____

   b. (consequently) _____

   _____

4. Many workers died quite young because they suffered accidents and injuries.

   a. (so) _____

   _____

   b. (as a result) _____

   _____

5. The upper classes avoided "playing around" because they were in the public eye.

a. (for) _____

_____

b. (therefore) _____

_____

⠿ **Part Five** Writing in the Academic World

Before Writing

A. Gathering Information.   You're going to write a paragraph about one of these wall paintings. In the chart that follows, fill in as much information as possible about these two paintings. If you don't know a piece of information, put a question mark.

Methethy with his Daughter and a Son, c. 2450 BC

Fragment of a wall painting from the tomb of Nebamun, Thebes, Egypt, c. 1450 BC

Elements	*Methethy with his Daughter and a Son*	Wall painting from the tomb of Nebamun
time: year and period (which kingdom?)		
use of space		
animals		
central figure (color, size, actions, style)		
adjectives to describe this work of art		

B. Applying Information.

1. Turn back to the Rules for Artists (page 110). How can the rules explain the depiction of figures in these two wall paintings?

   • *Methethy with his Daughter and a Son:* Reasons for the characteristics of the figures:

   _____

   _____

   _____

• Wall painting from the tomb of Nebamun: Reasons for the characteristics of the figures:

_____

_____

_____

2. In Part Three you read about three periods in Egyptian history (and art). How did each period influence the art?

_____

_____

_____

C. Choosing a Topic.   For the topic of your paragraph, choose one of the two paintings from your chart on page 130.

Writing

writing Strategy

Taking an Essay Exam

On an essay exam, you will need to answer one or more questions in complete paragraphs. The instructor wants to find out if you 1) have done the reading for the class, 2) understand it, and 3) can apply it to a new situation. Clearly, it is not enough simply to memorize information for an essay exam.

It's important to read the essay questions or directions carefully and stay on target in writing your paragraph. In other words, keep on the specific topic that the instructor has given. There are many possible directions on an essay exam. In this chapter we will examine essay questions that require a cause and effect paragraph. Notice in the following examples that often an essay "question" is not a question at all; instead, it is in the form of a command or directions.

Examples: Explain why . . .

Trace the causes of . . .

Identify the major reasons for . . .

Give three reasons for . . .

The following paragraph is one way to follow this direction:

> Briefly describe the figures on the Throne of Tutankhamen and identify reasons for their naturalness or unnaturalness.

Example: The figures on Tutankhamen's magnificent throne seem somewhat unnatural to the modern observer because the artist was following the strict rules for artists in ancient Egypt. These figures are depictions of the pharaoh and his queen, so they appear inactive and unmoving to show their high status. The queen appears in this piece of tomb art to be with her husband for all eternity. Since her figure is the same size as her husband's, we can assume that she was considered his equal in status. Egyptian religion required artists to depict all parts of the body from the most familiar point of view. Consequently, we see the feet, arms, and head of these figures in profile and their shoulders and eye from the front. Also, arms and legs of both people are clearly shown so that their ka can live forever in a complete body. This throne was created in the New Kingdom, not long after the time of Ikhnaton, and it is clear that there is some influence from the naturalness of art at that time. For example, the pharaoh almost casually hooks his right arm over the back of the throne, and in a charming gesture, the queen has bent toward her husband to touch him on the shoulder. As a result, both figures appear less stiff, less frozen than most figures in earlier periods of Egyptian art.

Notice in the example:

1. The topic sentence both very generally describes the figures ("somewhat unnatural") and gives the general reason for this unnaturalness ("strict rules for artists").

2. There is a lot of support for the topic sentence.

3. The paragraph stays on target. It deals only with the figures—not with the use of space or details around the figures.

4. There is a variety of transitional words of cause and effect and purpose.

Writing Assignment: First Draft.   Choose *one* of these essay questions and write a paragraph about either *Methethy with his Daughter and a Son* or fragment of a wall painting from the tomb of Nebamun. Use your notes on the chart on page 130 to help you organize your ideas.

- Explain the use of space in this painting. How did the artist fill the space and for what reasons?

- Briefly describe the animal and human figures in the painting and give reasons for the style.

- Give a brief description of the figures in the painting and identify reasons for their style.

After Writing

A. Self-Check.   Read over your paragraph. Answer the questions on the following checklist. Write *yes* or *no*.

B. Classmate's Check.   Exchange papers with a classmate. Check each other's paragraphs. Write *yes* or *no* on your classmate's checklist.

editing Checklist

Points To Check For	My Check	My Classmate's Check
1. Is the paragraph form correct (indentation, margins)?		
2. Is the piece of art mentioned in the topic sentence?		
3. Are clear reasons given?		
4. Is there correct use of transition words?		
5. Is there variety in the use of transitions?		
6. Other: _____		

Second Draft.   Use the answers on your checklist to guide you in your revision. Rewrite your paragraph and give it to your teacher.

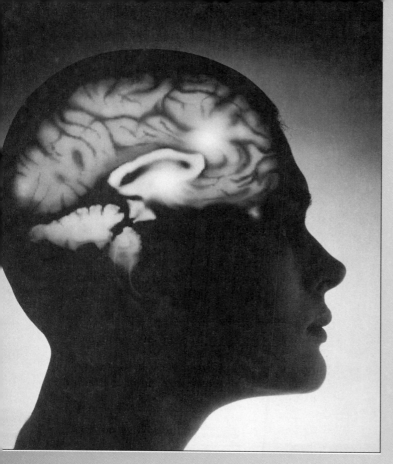

unit
3

Psychology

chapter Five

States of Consciousness

Is it possible to be conscious while dreaming and direct our dreams? How do people in different cultures interpret dreams? What do our dreams mean? In this chapter we will explore the mysterious world of dreaming.

Part One Lucid Dreaming

Before Reading

A. Discussion.   Look at these ads from a catalog. With a partner, answer these questions.

1. From the first ad, what can you guess that *lucid dreaming* is?

2. Why would someone buy a *dream catcher*?

Home-Study Guide to Lucid Dreaming

Would you like to remember your dreams, to experience the joy of flying in your nightly dreams? Can you imagine *knowing* when you are dreaming and becoming a "director" of your dreams? Learn to explore the world of your dreams! Become a lucid dreamer with this 3-month program.

How to Become a Lucid Dreamer
(Order # MHC 9697) $59.00

Dream Catcher

American Indians place a "dream catcher" over their beds at night. The net is believed to catch nightmares and protect sleepers from these bad dreams. It also attracts good dreams and helps the dreamer remember them! Made by Native Americans in the Southwest.

Dream Catcher
(Order # MHC 9798) $15.99

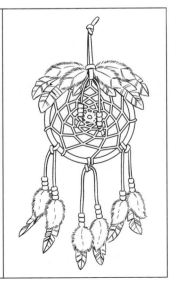

B. Thinking Ahead.   In small groups, answer this question: Do you do any of the following?

- remember your dreams?
- talk about dreams with friends or family?
- have flying dreams?
- think, "This is just a dream" while you're dreaming?
- write down your dreams?

Reading

As you read the following passage, look for the answers to these questions.

1. What can a dreamer do in lucid dreaming?

2. How can a person become a lucid dreamer?

Lucid Dreaming

The History of Lucid Dreaming

In a lucid dream, the dreamer becomes consciously aware that he or she is dreaming while participating in the events and emotions of the dream. As far back as the fourth century BC,
5 Aristotle commented: "Often when one is asleep, there is something . . . which declares that what . . . presents itself is . . . a dream." Lucid dreams were given a special status in early Christianity, Tibetan Buddhism, and Islam.

10   In England, Oliver Fox independently discovered lucid dreaming in 1902. He called lucid dreams "dreams of knowledge." In such dreams, Fox felt "free as air, secure in the . . . knowledge that I could always wake if danger threatened."

15   Several [modern] popular books have focused attention on lucid dreaming. Patricia Garfield had a chapter on lucid dreams in *Creative Dreaming* (1974). She wrote that the lucid dreamer would have an "unbelievable freedom
20 from all restrictions of body, time, and space":

When you become lucid you can do *anything* in your dream. You can fly anywhere you wish, . . . converse with friends long dead or people unknown to
25 you; you can see any place in the world you choose, experience all levels of positive emotions, receive answers to questions, . . . observe creative products, and, in general, use the full
30 resources of the material stored in your mind. *You can learn to become conscious during your dreams.*

Techniques for Developing Lucidity

Stephen LaBerge, at the Stanford University Sleep Lab, has developed a method called the
35 MILD technique (Mnemonic Induction of Lucid Dreams). This involves waking up from a dream, imagining yourself back in that same dream, seeing yourself becoming lucid, and telling yourself, "Next time I'm dreaming, I want to

40 recognize I'm dreaming." LaBerge claims that with practice using his MILD technique, he was able to have lucid dreams on any night he wished.

To gain access to your dreams, you don't 45 have to exert any physical energy. The only mental energy required is that of paying attention to the dreams that are given to you and being willing to consider the possible messages.

You can start your preparation today by find- 50 ing a notebook or diary to record your dreams tomorrow morning. Place it on your nightstand or under your pillow tonight.

When you wake up during the night or in the morning, don't open your eyes immediately. Lie 55 very still and try gently to recall any imagery.

Were you in some building or unusual location? Was anyone else present? Did you notice something unusual? If you can recall any specific image (D), try to reconnect it with whatever event 60 or activity preceded it (C), and what preceded that (B), and what preceded that (A). Think about these events or images a few times before opening your eyes and recording the dream in its ABCD order. Describe the dream as fully as you 65 can without crossing out any words.

As you begin to experience the personal rewards of your dream explorations, your dream journal will achieve a special place in your life. Review your journal from time to time to note 70 how your life patterns are changing. Good journeying!

Source: "Lucid Dreaming" adapted from Robert Van de Castle, *Our Dreaming Mind*, pp. 440–467. Copyright © 1994 by Robert Van de Castle, Ph.D. Adapted and reprinted with the permission of Ballantine Books, a division of Random House, Inc.

After Reading

A. Main Ideas.   Go back and answer the two questions on page 139. Mark the sentences in the reading passage where you found the answers.

B. Point of View.   Does the writer of *Lucid Dreaming* believe that it's *good* or *bad* to be a lucid dreamer? Look through the passage quickly and mark the adjectives and phrases that support your answer.

C. Discussion.   In small groups, talk for a few minutes about your reactions to *Lucid Dreaming*.

1. Had you heard of lucid dreaming before?

2. What do you think about it?

3. If you have had flying dreams before, tell your group about one.

4. If you have had lucid dreams, tell your group about one.

D. Application.   For the next week (beginning tonight), keep a notebook and pen beside your bed. When you wake from a dream, write it down quickly before you forget it. *Bring these dream reports to class each day. You might want to use them in your writing in Part Five.*

E. Response Writing.   Think about one dream that you have had recently or in the past. Choose from this list:

- a good dream or a nightmare

- a lucid dream or a flying dream

- a recurring dream (one that you've had many times)

For ten minutes, write about this dream. Don't stop writing to use a dictionary or to worry about grammar.

. : : : : : : Part Two Dreaming across Cultures

Before Reading

A. Discussion.   The reading passage in this section explains beliefs about dreams in four different cultures. Before you read, in small groups discuss what *your* culture believes about dreams. When you finish your discussion, share your answers with the rest of the class.

1. Do people think that dreams are important? Do they talk about the meaning of dreams? Do some people take dreams more seriously than others do?

2. What do most people think that dreams mean? What are some folk beliefs (traditional ideas) about the meaning of dreams? In other words, what did your grandparents or great-grandparents believe about dreaming?

B. Vocabulary Preparation.   The reading contains some new words, but try not to use a dictionary. You can guess the meaning of most new words from

- the context

- stems and affixes

- your own knowledge of the situation

Before reading, do this exercise with the following underlined words that you will find later in the passage. Fill in the blanks with your own words that have the same meaning as the underlined words.

1. In ancient times, when people were sick and wanted to be <u>healed</u>, they went to special healing centers.

    When people are sick, they want to be _____.

2. In some religions, an animal is <u>sacrificed</u> before or during a ceremony. What happens to an animal in some religious ceremonies?

It is _____.

3. He acted as an <u>intermediary</u> between the angry workers and the employers during the strike last year.

If two people or groups don't speak directly, what do they need someone to do? _____

_____

4. Everyone is hoping that scientists will soon find a <u>cure</u> for cancer and other terrible sicknesses.

We want (a) _____ for cancer.

5. The police are <u>seeking</u> information about a lost child; they have no idea, yet, what happened to her.

When a child is lost, the police _____ information.

6. When we go on our hike in the mountains next weekend, Alan is going to <u>guide</u> us because it's easy to get lost in that area.

What will Alan do to help us? _____

C. Thinking Ahead. Look quickly over the Comprehension Check on page 145 before you read. It usually helps to have a few questions in mind as you read.

Reading

As you read the following passage, mark any information that seems important to you.

Dreaming across Cultures

The ancient Greeks looked to their dreams to guide them to good health. When they were sick and wanted to be healed, they went to the
5 temple of Asklepios, the god of healing. They paid for an animal—a chicken, goat, or sheep—to be sacrificed. Then they slept on the temple floor in the belief that the god would come to them in a dream and
10 tell them what to do in order to be cured.

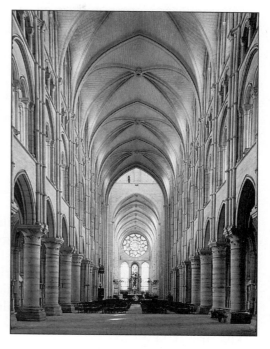

Over a thousand years later, during the Middle Ages, the tradition continued. European Christians used to sleep in churches in the hopes of having a dream to
15 cure their sickness. The Church, however, did not approve of this practice. The Church saw itself as the intermediary between God and people. If people could listen to God directly, in their dreams, then
20 the power of the Church was lessened.

Until very recently, the Senoi people of Malaysia were famous for their art of dream interpretation. Each day, adults used to meet with each other to discuss
25 their dreams in order to solve personal and community problems. At breakfast every day, children told their dreams to older family members and learned dream interpretation in the discussion and analysis
30 that followed. Children learned to use their dreams creatively and change feelings of ill will—fear, anger, or hatred—into

people's traditions may seek a vision—a rare and special kind of dream—in two ways: through the use of *peyote* or through a *vision quest*. Peyote is a kind of drug from the cactus plant. When people eat it as part of a religious ceremony, sometimes they experience visions of God or Jesus or a spirit. Their visions are associated with images from their specific cultures. A Mexican Indian, for example, might see beautiful colored birds. An Indian from the flatlands of the United States might envision buffalo. In a vision quest, people suffer hunger, physical pain, and loneliness for several days in an attempt to have a vision that will guide them or their people.

feelings of good will. For example, if a child had a nightmare about falling, his elders told him that it was a wonderful dream; it was the quickest way to contact the spirit world, and there was nothing to be afraid of. In his next falling dream, he should relax and see where the dream might take him. If a child dreamed that she was attacking someone, she needed to apologize to that person and share something good with him. The goal was for dreamers to gain control of their dream world and then the waking world. In this way, the Senoi lived peacefully within themselves and their society, without psychological problems, crime, or violence.

Dreams have always been important in Native American culture, too, but in quite a different way from the Senoi. Indians in North America who follow their

After Reading

A. Comprehension Check: Synthesizing Information. On a piece of paper, answer these questions.

1. How were the Christians of the Middle Ages similar in their dream life to the ancient Greeks? How were they different?

2. What do some traditional Native Americans do in their dream life that is different from the other cultures in the reading selection?

B. General and Specific Ideas. Which sentence in each group is the most general of the three? Put a check mark by it. Put an S by all of the specific information that supports the general idea.

1. the ancient Greeks

     _S_   slept on the temple floor

     _√_   looked to their dreams to guide them to good health

     _S_   believed that Asklepios came to them in their dreams

2. Christians of the Middle Ages

     _____   looked to their dreams to guide them to good health

     _____   continued the tradition that was begun by the Greeks

     _____   slept in churches

3. Senoi adults

     _____   taught dream interpretation to their children

     _____   worked to gain control of their dream world and then the waking world

     _____   discussed their dreams with each other in order to solve personal and community problems

4. Native Americans

     _____   took a drug called peyote

     _____   went through vision quests

     _____   wanted to have visions to guide them or their people

C. Vocabulary Expansion.   Your vocabulary will grow faster if you learn different parts of speech when you learn a new word. Use the reading selection and a dictionary to fill in these blanks.

Nouns	Verbs	Adjectives
1. intermediary	_____	_____
2. cure	_____	_____
3. interpretation	_____	_____
4. vision	_____	_____
5. sacrifice	_____	_____

. : : : : :   **Part Three** Reading in the Academic World

Before Reading

A. Vocabulary Preparation.   The following textbook selection contains words that will be new to you. Guess the meaning of some of these from the contexts that follow. When you write your guess, be sure to use the same part of speech as that of the underlined word. After you guess the meaning, check with a dictionary to see if your guess was close.

1. According to Freud's theory, we dream for wish <u>fulfillment</u> to satisfy unconscious desires or wishes.

   My Guess: _____

   Dictionary Definition: _____

2. In the day <u>preceding</u> her wedding, she was both excited and nervous.

   My Guess: _____

   Dictionary Definition: _____

3. On Halloween, the children <u>disguised</u> themselves as ghosts, Superman, and cartoon heroes.

   My Guess: _____

   Dictionary Definition: _____

4. He doesn't have many <u>tasks</u> this morning. He just needs to type a few letters, make some photo copies, and go to the post office.

   My Guess: _____

   Dictionary Definition: _____

5. I closed my eyes and pointed to a place on the map. In this way, I decided at <u>random</u> where to go.

My Guess: _____

Dictionary Definition: _____

6. After several years of work, the scientist sadly <u>acknowledged</u> publicly that there had been mistakes in his experiment.

My Guess: _____

Dictionary Definition: _____

7. When I first moved into this house, I had only a bed, two chairs, and one table. It looked very empty. The furniture was <u>sparse</u>.

My Guess: _____

Dictionary Definition: _____

reading Strategy

Choosing the Correct Dictionary Definition

Some words have just one meaning. Many words, however, have more than one meaning. When you use a dictionary, you need to find the definition that *fits the context in which you found the word.* First, determine the part of speech of the word. Then look at each definition of the word in the dictionary. Look back and forth from the sentence to the dictionary to see which definition is the correct one. Be sure to read the dictionary examples of how to use the word; sometimes these help you more than the definitions.

Examples: The police are <u>seeking</u> information about the missing child.

> *you can stop her.*
> **seek** /siʸk/ *v* **sought** /sɔt/, **seeking 1** [I; T *after, for, out*] *fml* to make a search (for); try to find or get (something): *He sought out his friend in the crowd.* |*to seek (after) the truth| seek public office* **2** [T] *fml* to ask for; go to request: *You should seek advice from your lawyer.* **3** [T +*to-v*] *lit* to try; make an attempt: *They sought to punish him for his crime but he escaped.* –**seeker** *n*
> **seem** /siʸm/ *v* **1** [+*to-v;* not *be+v-ing*] to give the idea or effect of being; appear: *She al-ways seems (to be) sad. |I seem to have caught*

You see that Definition 1 is close. Definition 3 doesn't fit at all. Definition 2 is the correct one for *seek* in this context.

Source: Dictionary entry for "seek" from *Longman Dictionary of American English,* page 614. Copyright © 1983 by Longman, Inc. Reprinted with the permission of Addison Wesley Longman.

B. Vocabulary Preparation: Dictionary Use.   As you did in Exercise A, guess the meaning of each underlined word. Then check with a dictionary to see if your guess was correct. Focus on choosing the correct definition. Then compare your answers with another student's.

1. Carl Jung <u>held that</u> dreams are symbolic in a very individual way, and many psychologists agree with this belief.

   My Guess: _____

   Dictionary Definition: _____

2. When the elevator broke down, it suddenly fell six floors, and the workers had to climb carefully down through the <u>shaft</u> to fix it.

   My Guess: _____

   Dictionary Definition: _____

3. She had to <u>face</u> a lot of problems when she moved to a new country.

   My Guess: _____

   Dictionary Definition: _____

C. Thinking Ahead.   The textbook selection presents three theories (ideas) about the meaning of dreams. It begins with a young man's dream. In his dream, he is in an elevator and begins kissing a young woman. Some parents get on the elevator, and it becomes shaky. He thinks the elevator will crash or get stuck. Why do you think he had this dream? What might the various elements represent? What might psychologists say about this dream?

Reading

As you read the textbook selection, mark any sentences that answer the following question and lead you to the main idea.

• What are three (or possibly four) different theories about the meaning of dreams?

Interpretation of Dreams

I am in an elevator sitting by myself against the wall. A girl comes in, and I say, "Come sit by me," and she sits by me (I don't even know her). I lean over and
5 start to kiss her. Then these parents get on the elevator and the elevator is real shaky, and I think that the elevator will crash or get stuck (adapted from Cohen, 1979).

Let's look at three theories about what this
10 dream might mean.

According to *Freud's theory,* we dream for wish fulfillment—to satisfy unconscious desires or wishes, especially those involving sex or aggression. These wishes cannot be
15 fulfilled during waking hours because they would create too much guilt or anxiety. Sigmund Freud believed that dreams contain experiences of preceding days as well as memories of early childhood.

20 Because dreams may contain wishes that make us anxious, Freud (1900) held that we disguise these wishes with symbols. For instance, he thought that long objects, such as an elevator shaft or a cigar, represented

25 male sex organs and that circular objects or empty spaces represented female sex organs. He saw the therapist's task as interpreting these symbols and helping the client discover his or her fearful and unconscious
30 desires, needs, and feelings. According to Freudian theory, the "elevator dream" suggests that the young man may have difficulties with sexual and parental relationships.

Many therapists agree with Freud that
35 dreams can represent past, present, or future concerns, fears, or worries. However, therapists disagree over how much of a dream's content is symbolic or disguised wishes and desires.

40 Disagreeing completely with Freud, researchers J. Alan Hobson and Robert W. McCarley (1977) proposed their *activation-synthesis theory,* which says that dreaming is

nothing more than random and meaningless
45 activity of nerve cells in the brain. According to their idea, an area in the pons sends
millions of random nerve impulses to the
cortex. In turn, the cortex tries to make sense
of these random signals by creating feelings,

50 imagined movements, changing scenes, and
meaningless images that we define as
dreams. From their viewpoint, there would
be no reason to interpret the elevator dream,
since it represents random activity of neu-
55 rons and not unconscious wishes or desires.

Hobson (1988) has revised this dream
theory to acknowledge that dreams may
have deep personal meaning. He now believes that the images and feelings that our
60 cortex imposes on millions of incoming neu-
ral signals reflect our past memories and
own personal view of the world.

Agreeing partly with Freud, many
therapists and sleep-dream researchers be-
65 lieve that dreams are *extensions of waking life*,
including thoughts and concerns, especially
emotional ones. Rosalind Cartwright (1988)
says, "The problem most therapists face is
that patients' dream material is sparse and
70 incomplete. People simply don't remember
their dreams very well. The therapist's task
is often like trying to reconstruct a 500-page
manuscript from just the last page. But
dreams collected from a single night in the
75 sleep lab read like chapters in a book. They
illuminate current concerns and the feelings
attached to them."

For example, she found that the dreams
of people undergoing divorce seem to be
80 about past marital problems; in contrast, the
dreams of those who are happily married
reflect many themes. In one sense, Cartwright is updating Freud's idea that dreams
are the "royal road to the unconscious." She
85 studies dreams in a sleep laboratory, and like
Freud, she would see the elevator dream as
providing clues to the person's problems,
concerns, and emotions.

Source: "Interpretation of Dreams" adapted from Rod Plotnik, *Introduction to Psychology, Third Edition,* page 172. Copyright © 1993 by
Wadsworth, Inc. Adapted and reprinted with the permission of Brooks/Cole Publishing Company, a division of Thomson Publishing Inc.,
511 Forest Lodge Road, Pacific Grove, CA 93950-5040.

After Reading

A. Main Ideas.   Go back to the reading. Use the points that you've marked to help you fill in the following chart.

Psychologist	Year	Theory about Dream Interpretation
Sigmund Freud		

B. Comprehension Check: Synthesizing Information.   Look at your chart. In your mind, compare the different theories of dream interpretation.

1. Which theories are most similar to each other? In what ways are they similar?

2. Which theories are very different from each other?

C. Application.   With a partner, analyze the three dreams that follow. Interpret each dream according to the theories in the reading. (How do you think Freud would interpret these dreams? What would Hobson and McCarley say? What would Cartwright say?)

Dream #1   I'm going into a thick forest. There are so many trees that it's hard to see very far. I decide to climb a tree to try to see better. It's difficult to climb, and I'm going really slowly. Finally, just as I get close to the top of the tree, I slip and fall down, down, down. I'm more scared than I've ever been. I know I'm going to die. Then I wake up.

—dream of an 18-year-old male student

Dream #2   I'm at work. Someone has found a baby fox. I'm amazed that this wild animal is here, in a city. It's a perfect creature but in miniature—just one-inch long. (I don't seem to notice the impossibility of this.) There are three evil scientists who are excited about this animal. They want to raise it and then do terrible experiments on it some day. I'm so angry, so furious, that I can't express myself. I take the baby fox and run away. I put the animal in my purse to keep it safe. I decide to take it up into the mountains and let it go free where it will be safe. As I'm climbing the mountain, my husband joins me. We pass farms and parks and lots of people. We have to find the wilderness. Finally, near the top, we stop to rest at a university. When I open my purse to check on the fox, he isn't there. I absolutely panic. He can't be gone! I was so careful! I look everywhere, but he's gone. I'll never find him.

—dream of a 40-year-old professional woman

Dream #3   I'm at a conference in Europe. It's been pleasant. One evening, we are invited to a dinner party at the home of a wealthy woman in Vienna. We walk into the home, which is incredibly beautiful. It's a combination of a castle, museum, and art gallery. There is rich, dark wood and Old Masters' paintings everywhere. I've never seen such art in a private home before. We are in a huge, elegant dining room, where waiters serve many courses of fabulous food. There is so much to see. I keep turning around to watch the people and see the art. I realize that I'm missing out on some of the food because others at my table take it while I'm marveling at the art. But this doesn't bother me because this experience is so special. I'm completely happy.

—dream of a 66-year-old retired man

⠿ **Part Four** The Mechanics of Writing

In Part Five, you are going to write two paragraphs—one of narration (about a dream) and one of analysis. You will need to use transition words of time in the paragraph of narration. You will need to use expressions to explain symbols in the paragraph of analysis. Part Four will help you to use these correctly.

Using Transition Words of Time

When you tell a story in *chronological* order (order of time), you may need to use transitional words of time. In Chapter Four you learned rules for the use of subordinating conjunctions of cause and effect. Here are some of the subordinating conjunctions of *time*.

Subordinating Conjunctions:

when	before
while	after
as (= while)	as soon as (= immediately after)

Examples: I was relieved *when* I woke up.   (Note: no comma)

When I woke up, I was relieved.   (Note: comma)

I couldn't remember the dream *after* I woke up.

After I woke up, I couldn't remember the dream.

Use:

1. There is a comma after the first clause if the sentence begins with the subordinating conjunction. There is no comma if the subordinating conjunction is in the middle.

2. *While* and *as* are often used with continuous tenses:

   As I *was running,* I wondered who was chasing me.

In Chapter Two you learned how to use adverbial conjunctions. Here is a brief review of adverbial conjunctions of *time.*

Adverbial Conjunctions:

first	finally
second	then
third (etc.)	afterwards

Examples: I had an awful nightmare last night. *Afterwards,* I couldn't remember the details, but I remember the feeling.

I was trying to run from a murderer when I felt a hand on my shoulder. *Then* I woke up.

There are several things you can do to become a lucid dreamer; *first,* you need to learn to value your dreams.

Use: Adverbial conjunctions often begin a sentence or independent clause. There is a period or semicolon before the adverbial conjunction. There is a comma after it (except for *then*).

A. Sentence Combining: Conjunctions.   Combine the following pairs of sentences as indicated. Use adverbial and subordinating conjunctions.

1. Lucid dreamers know that they're dreaming.

The dream is happening. (*while*)

_____

_____

2. You need to replay the dream in your mind.

You open your eyes. (*before*)

_____

_____

3. He realized that it was only a dream.

A dream enemy was chasing him. (*as*)

_____

_____

4. Replay the dream in your mind.

Open your eyes and write it down. (*then*)

_____

_____

5. Greeks were sick.

They went to the temple of Asklepios. (*when*)

_____

_____

6. You should focus on thoughts of flying during the day.

You need to think about past flying dreams at night. (*first/second*)

_____

_____

Narration

A *narrative* is a story. When we tell a story, we usually use the past tense. However, when we describe a *dream* in English, we use mostly the simple present tense, with some present continuous, present perfect, and future.

B. Identifying Tenses.   Notice the use of tenses in the following narrative of a dream. Mark each tense with a felt-tip pen.

> I go into my uncle's office. It's late at night, after hours. Nobody is there. I haven't come to take anything. I'm just curious. I look around and find it uninteresting. I'm moving from room to room. I notice that it's not a beautiful office at all, just functional. I notice with shock that there are video cameras hanging from the ceiling. There are several of them, and they're following me. I'm going from one room to another. I'm terrified and want to escape. I try to hide under a desk, but I know the cameras have already caught me.

Writing about Symbols

Sigmund Freud, Carl Jung, and other psychologists have taught that dreams have meaning and are associated with conscious thoughts and problems. They pointed out that dreams are filled with *symbols*. Jung believed that "dreams are highly individualized," so the same symbol might have a different meaning to different people. However, some symbols seem to be universal; in other words, they appear to have the same meaning to people everywhere. We see them in art, religion, and dreams. To write about symbols (for example, in a psychology, anthropology, or literature class), it is useful to know a variety of expressions to explain them. Here are a few.

Noun		Noun
Light	**is a symbol of**	understanding or knowledge.
The ankh (☥)	**is symbolic of**	life, the universe, and man.
A flag	**represents**	a country.
A circle	**is associated with**	the self and wholeness.
Snakes around a staff	**symbolize**	medicine.

C. Writing about Symbols.

What do the following symbols mean to you? (There are no "right" or "wrong" answers.) On a piece of paper, write a complete sentence for each symbol. Use structures from the preceding box.

Example: I think a road is symbolic of a person's life.

1. a road
2. a star
3. an owl
4. a cross

5. five interconnected rings
6. breath
7. water
8. a crescent

When you finish your sentences, compare your answers with those of other students. Were your answers similar or different?

D. Talking about Symbols.

Move around the classroom. Ask your classmates about each of the symbols on the following chart and fill in their answers. Add any others that you can think of. Ask questions such as these:

- What does the color red represent to you?
- What does a road symbolize to you?
- What do you think an eagle is symbolic of?

Symbol	Person	Meaning	Person	Meaning
1. red				
2. a road				
3. an eagle				
4. water				
5. a dove				
6. a river				

Symbol	Person	Meaning	Person	Meaning
7. a door				
8. twins				
9. a key				
10. the ocean				
11. green				
12. a mirror				

When you finish, write twelve sentences based on your chart. Use the five structures from the box on page 155.

Example: To Anne, the color red is associated with danger.

·:::: **Part Five** Writing in the Academic World

Before Writing

A. Gathering Information.   Interview three classmates. Ask each of them these questions and take careful notes of their answers.

1. What was one of your most memorable dreams?

2. What was happening in your life at the time you had this dream?

3. What does this dream mean to you?

B. Choosing a Topic.   In most writing assignments, your teacher will give you some choice of topic, within limits. *It's important for you to choose carefully a topic that you enjoy and have some ideas about.* To prepare for the writing assignment in this chapter, choose one dream that interests you. This should be a dream that you think you can interpret. It's best to work with one of your *own recent* dreams because the symbols may have a personal meaning to you. However, you could choose another person's dream or a dream from your past, instead.

Choose **one** of the following:

- the dream from your Response Writing in Part One

- one of the dreams that you wrote down during the week

- any dream that you can remember well

- Dream #3 on page 152

- a dream of one of your classmates from your interviews

C. Idea Mapping.   On a piece of paper, make a map of the dream that you've chosen. Put the theme (subject) at the center and important details around it.

Example: This is how the dreamer of #2 on page 152 might map it.

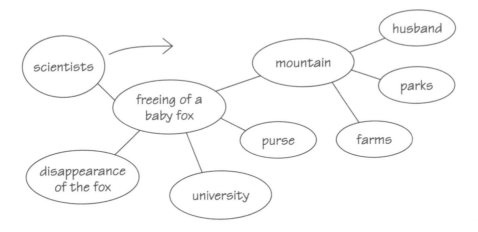

D. Analysis of Details.   What do you think your dream represents? On another page, make quick notes on the theme and any details that you think you understand. Don't worry about the other details and don't worry about being "right" or "wrong."

Example:

freeing of a fox = desire for motherhood	purse = my body, womb
scientists = ???	university = my professional goals
mountain = my life	disappearance of the fox = knowing
farms, parks = ???	that I won't have children

Writing

writing Strategy

Organizing a Paragraph of Analysis

In a paragraph of *narration,* you tell a story, so the actions are in the order of time. (See pages 153–155 for examples.)

   One way to organize a paragraph of *analysis* is to begin with the topic sentence (and main idea), then examine each detail, and end with a sentence of conclusion. To be more persuasive, you can add reasons.

Example: My dream about freeing the baby fox is, I think, about my desire to have a child because in the dream I felt protective and maternal toward the fox. } topic sentence

The mountain is symbolic of my life, and the fact that my husband joined me symbolizes our marriage. Freud would say that the purse is a "female symbol," and I think this is probably true. It's an "empty space," and I put the fox in it to keep it safe. The university represents education. To me, it is associated with my profession. I've worked for many years to reach this level in my work, and I haven't left much room in my life for a child. } details

For this reason, it seems clear that "losing" the animal means that I know, unconsciously, that I won't have children. } conclusion

Notice in the paragraph above that the details are also in chronological order because it is the analysis of a dream, a narrative.

A. Organizing Information.   Go back to your notes of analysis about the details in your dream. Put these details in chronological order. Write 1, 2, 3, etc. next to each part of your dream that you understand.

writing Strategy

Using Variety in Language

If you need to say the same thing several times in a paragraph, try not to use the exact same words each time. Try to use synonyms, instead.

B. Analysis.   Read the preceding paragraph again. In how many ways does the writer say "means"? Mark each way with a felt-tip pen.

Writing Assignment: First Draft.   Write two paragraphs. The first will be a *narrative*—the story of your dream. Because it is a dream, use mainly present tenses in this paragraph. The second paragraph will be your *analysis* of the dream.

After Writing

A. Self-Check.   Read over your paragraphs and answer the questions on the following checklist. Write yes or no.

B. Classmate's Check.   Exchange papers with a classmate. Check each other's paragraphs. Write yes or no on your classmate's checklist.

editing Checklist

Points To Check For	My Check	My Classmate's Check
First paragraph:		
1. Is the paragraph in chronological order?	_____	_____
2. Are the transition words used correctly?	_____	_____
3. Are tenses used correctly in the paragraph?	_____	_____
Second paragraph:		
4. Does the topic sentence give the theme of the dream?	_____	_____
5. Are the details in chronological order (the same order as in the first paragraph)?	_____	_____
6. Is there variety in the phrases of representation?	_____	_____
7. Are some reasons given for the symbols that were chosen?	_____	_____
8. Other: _____	_____	_____

Second Draft.   Use the answers on your checklist to guide you in your revision. Rewrite your paragraphs and give them to your teacher.

chapter Six

Abnormal Psychology

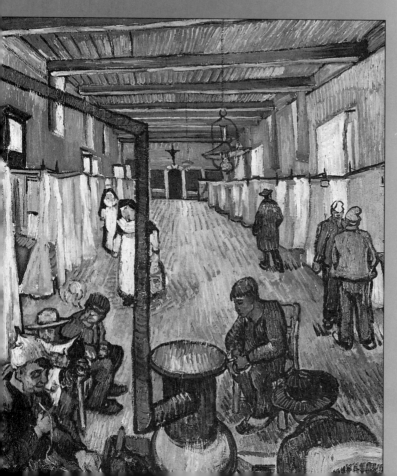

What psychological problems do you already know about? How does culture influence psychology? What are some ways in which psychologists treat their patients? In this chapter we will study *abnormal psychology*.

.∴:::: **Part One** What Is Abnormal?

Before Reading

Look at these photos. With a partner, answer the questions that follow.

1. Which of these people might have psychological problems? What kinds of problems might they have?

2. Why did you choose the people that you did?

3. Can you name any psychological problems? What are their symptoms?

a.

b.

c.

d.

e.

f.

g.

h.

j.

i.

Reading

As you read the following passage, look for answers to these questions.

1. What are three ways of defining abnormality?

2. Four psychological disorders are mentioned—the only disorders that are found in all cultures of the world. What are they?

What Is Abnormal?

A man living in the Ozark Mountains has a vision in which God speaks to him. He begins preaching to his relatives and neighbors, and soon he has the whole town in a state of religious fervor. People say that God has "called" him to speak to them. He becomes famous as a prophet and healer, and in time he is drawing large audiences everywhere he goes. However, when he goes into the city of St. Louis and attempts to hold a prayer meeting on a main street at rush hour, blocking traffic, he is arrested. He tells the policemen about his conversations with God, and they hurry him off to the nearest mental hospital.

A housewife is tired all the time, but she has trouble sleeping. Her housework keeps piling up because she has no energy to do it. Applications for adult classes and ads from the newspaper for jobs lie in a drawer, untouched. She goes to her family doctor, but he says she's in perfect health. One night she tells her husband that she's thinking of seeing a psychotherapist. He thinks this is ridiculous—stupid. According to him, all she needs is to get up out of her chair and get busy.

What Is Abnormal Behavior?

Who is right? The "prophet" or the policemen? The housewife or her husband? It is often difficult to draw a line between normal and abnormal behavior. Behavior that some people consider normal seems abnormal to others. One approach to abnormality is to say that whatever most people do is normal. Abnormality, then, is any deviation from the average or from the majority. If most people cheat on their income taxes, are honest taxpayers abnormal? If most people are noncreative, was Shakespeare abnormal? Because the majority is not always right or best, this approach to defining abnormality is not generally useful.

Another way to distinguish normal from abnormal people is to say that normal people
25 are able to get along in the world—physically, emotionally, and socially. They can feed and
clothe themselves, work, find friends, and live by the rules of society. By this definition,
abnormal people are the ones who cannot *adjust.* They may be so unhappy that they refuse
to eat or are so tired that they cannot hold a job. They may experience so much anxiety
in relationships with others that they end up avoiding people, living in a lonely world of
30 their own.

The terms "mental illness" and "mental health" imply that psychological disturbance
or abnormality is like a physical sickness—such as the flu or tuberculosis. Although many
psychologists think that "mental illness" is different from physical illness, the idea remains that there is some ideal ("perfect") way for people to function psychologically, just
35 as there is an ideal way for people to function physically. The fact that it is difficult to define
abnormality does not mean that no such thing exists. It does mean that we should be
cautious about judging a person to be "mentally ill" just because he or she acts in a way
that we cannot understand. It should also be kept in mind that mild psychological disorders are common. It is only when a psychological problem becomes serious enough to
40 disrupt everyday life that it becomes an "abnormality" or "illness."

Anxiety-Based Disorders

Fifteen percent of adults have symptoms typical of the anxiety-based disorders. People
with these disorders are deeply anxious and seem unable to free themselves of worries and
fears. When severe (serious) anxiety is focused on a particular object, activity, or situation
that seems out of proportion to the real dangers involved, it is called a **phobia.** Phobias
45 may be classified as simple phobias, social phobias, and agoraphobia. A *simple phobia*
can focus on almost anything, including high places (acrophobia), enclosed spaces (claus-
trophobia), and darkness (nyctophobia). Victims of social phobias fear that they will
embarrass themselves in a public place or social setting. People suffering from an extreme
fear of crowds (*agoraphobia*) may stop going to movies or shopping in large, busy stores.
50 Some reach the point where they will not leave their houses at all. Phobias may be mild
or extremely severe. Most people deal with their phobias by avoiding the thing that fright-
ens them.

Mood Disorders

We all experience mood swings. Sometimes we are happy, while at other times we feel
miserable or depressed. Occasional depression is a common experience. In some people,
55 however, these moods are more intense and last longer. These individuals often get the
sense that their depression will go on forever and that there is nothing they can do to
change it.

Major depressive disorder is a pattern of sadness, anxiety, fatigue (tiredness), and reduced ability to function and interact with others. It may also interfere with sleep and
60 the ability to concentrate.

A common type of mood disorder is a **bipolar disorder,** in which individuals are excessively and inappropriately happy or unhappy. These reactions may take the form of high elation (excitement), hopeless depression, or an alternation between the two.

Schizophrenia

We can understand depression. Most of us have experienced anxiety. However, it is hard
65 to understand an individual with **schizophrenia,** who has lost contact with reality and lives life as an unreal dream. Schizophrenia is not a single problem; rather, it is a collection of symptoms. Many people with schizophrenia experience *delusions*—false beliefs—and *hallucinations* (seeing or hearing something that isn't really there).

Source: "What Is Abnormal?" adapted from Richard A. Kasschau, *Understanding Psychology,* pp. 363–378. Copyright © 1995 by Glencoe Publishing Company. Reprinted with the permission of the publishers.

After Reading

A. Main Ideas.   Go back and answer the two questions on page 164. Mark the sentences in the reading selection where you found the answers.

B. Application.   Look over these descriptions of four people. What might be each person's problem? Use the passage on pages 165–166 to help you identify each problem.

1. Aliki has felt deeply sad for over a month. She finds no pleasure in anything. She's tired all the time and has trouble remembering things. She doesn't want to eat and can't sleep well. She thinks a lot about her failures. She feels that everything she has ever done has been wrong and feels totally hopeless.

DISORDER: _____

2. Ben is a 34-year-old businessman who is terribly afraid of heights. This began several years ago. He had gone hiking with some people from the office at a time when he was feeling tense and anxious about family problems. At one point, when he was hiking up a steep mountain trail, he looked down and saw a river far, far below. He felt an intense wave of fear. This fear of high places has become more serious. Now he no longer goes to the mountains—which isn't a big problem for him—but he also cannot go above the fourth floor in any building—which *is* a problem, especially in his business.

DISORDER: _____

3. Maria is no longer able to go to work or carry out daily activities. She hears voices that command her to do things. She believes these voices come from outer space and must be obeyed. She has a strange, illogical use of language. She deeply distrusts all people in uniforms and believes they are trying to kill her.

DISORDER: _____

4. For several days Hong feels great, and he has enormous energy. He talks fast and has many, many ideas for new projects. It is a time of intense creativity. Then, suddenly, he loses all energy, becomes very sad, and feels completely hopeless.

DISORDER: _____

C. Discussion.   In a small group, discuss these questions.

1. In your opinion, how is a phobia different from a normal fear? What might be some "healthy fears"?

2. What are you afraid of? (High places? Crowds? Snakes? etc.) Can you think of when you first had this fear, and why? How do you deal with this fear?

3. Do you know anyone who is phobic? How does this phobia affect her or his life?

4. Do you know of any famous people who suffered from a psychological disorder? If so, who were they? Do you know what disorder they had?

D. Response Writing.   Choose *one* of the following questions to answer.

• What is one fear that you have, and how does it affect your life?

• What do *you* think is "abnormal"?

For ten minutes, write as much as you can in answering the question you chose. Don't stop writing to use a dictionary or to worry about grammar.

Part Two Abnormality—Culture Based?

Before Reading

A. Discussion.   The reading passage in this section deals with psychological disorders in several different cultures. Before you read, discuss *your* culture's views about psychological abnormality.

1. Is it common for people to seek the help of psychologists? How do people deal with abnormal behavior in a friend or relative?

2. Do you know of any psychological disorders that exist in some cultures but not in others?

B. Vocabulary Preparation.   The reading contains some new words, but try not to use a dictionary. You can guess the meaning of many new words from:

- the context

- your knowledge of the situation

Before reading, do this exercise, which introduces some of the words that you'll find. On each line, write a synonym or definition for the underlined word; choose from this list:

> something that the mind can clearly realize
>
> diseases; sicknesses
>
> dead
>
> abnormally concerned or worried about
>
> controlled; completely influenced
>
> believed; taken as truth even without proof

1. Is his grandfather still alive, or is he <u>deceased</u>?

   _____

2. She's <u>obsessed with</u> her weight; she worries constantly about her appearance.

   _____

3. His ideas on that subject are fairly <u>concrete</u>—clear, real, and specific.

   _____

4. In western society, it is <u>assumed</u> that a person who hears voices of dead people has a psychological disorder.

   _____

5. He suffers from both physical and psychological <u>maladies</u>.

   _____

6. In the horror movie *The Exorcist,* a little girl is <u>possessed</u> by a demon (evil spirit or devil) who takes over her mind and body.

   _____

C. Thinking Ahead. Look over the Comprehension Check on page 170 briefly before you read. It usually helps to have a few questions in mind as you read.

Reading

As you read, don't worry about the words that you don't know; instead, just try to understand the main idea and important details.

Abnormality—Culture Based?

In most people's view, a person who hears voices of the recently deceased is probably a victim of some psychological disturbance. Yet members of the Plains Indian tribe routinely hear the voices of the dead calling to them from the afterlife.

5   This is only one example of the role that culture plays in the labeling of behavior as "abnormal." In fact, of all the major adult disorders, just four are found across all cultures of the world: schizophrenia, bipolar disorder, major depression, and anxiety disorders.

Take, for instance, anorexia nervosa. This is a weight disorder in
10   which people, particularly women, develop inaccurate views of their body appearance, become obsessed with their weight, and refuse to eat, sometimes starving in the process. This disorder occurs only in cultures holding the societal standard that slender female bodies are most desirable. Because for most of the world such a standard does not exist,
15   anorexia nervosa does not occur. Interestingly, there is no anorexia nervosa in all of Asia, with two exceptions; the upper and upper-middle class of Japan and Hong Kong, where the influence of western culture tends to be great. It is also interesting that anorexia nervosa is a fairly recent disorder. In the 1600s and 1700s, it did not occur because the
20   ideal female body in western society at that time was a plump one.

Similarly, dissociative identity (multiple-personality) disorder only makes sense as a problem in societies in which a sense of self is fairly concrete. In places like India, the self is based more on factors external and relatively independent of the person. There, when an individual
25   displays symptoms of what people in western society would call multiple-personality disorder, it is assumed that this individual is possessed by demons (which is viewed as a malady) or by gods (which is not a cause for treatment).

Even though such disorders as schizo-
30 phrenia are found throughout the world, the
particular symptoms of the disorder are
influenced by cultural factors. Hence, catatonic schizophrenia, in which unmoving
patients appear to be frozen in the same
35 position sometimes for days, is rare in North
America and western Europe. In contrast, in
India, 80 percent of those with schizophrenia are catatonic.

Other cultures have disorders that do not
40 appear in the west. For example, in Malaysia, a behavior called "amok" is characterized
by a wild outburst in which a person, usually
quiet and withdrawn, kills or severely in-
jures another. Another example is a disorder
45 sometimes found in rural Japan—"kitsunet-suki"—in which those
afflicted think that they have been possessed by foxes and display facial
expressions characteristic of the animals.

Source: "Abnormality—Culture Based?"adapted from Robert S. Feldman, *Essentials of Understanding Psychology, Second Edition, International Edition*, page 448, Copyright © 1995 by by McGraw-Hill, Inc. Reprinted with the permission of the publishers.

After Reading

A. Comprehension Check: Main Idea.   Circle the number of the main idea of the reading passage.

1. Four disorders (schizophrenia, bipolar disorder, major depression, and anxiety disorders) are found in all cultures of the world.

2. Plains Indians suffer from schizophrenia because they hear the voices of deceased people.

3. Some psychological disorders appear only in western societies, others in the east.

4. Some psychological disorders—and the way in which people view them—seem to depend on culture.

B. Finding Important Details.   Fill in this chart with information from the reading. (It's not necessary to use complete sentences.) Work with a partner.

Disorder	Symptoms	Culture(s)	The Influence of Culture
dissociative identity (multiple-personality)		western society ----	seen as a disorder ----
		---- India	
amok			

C. Making Inferences.   Why do you think there are quotation marks around the word *abnormal* in the second paragraph?

D. Vocabulary Expansion: Stems and Affixes.   You can guess the meanings of some new words if you understand stems and affixes—word parts. Most of these come to English from Greek and Latin. There are many of them in the three readings in this chapter. Some are on the following list. Use this chart to help you figure out the meaning of each word in the list following the chart. Match the definitions to the words.

Prefixes	Meanings
ab-	not; away; off
an-	without
anti-	against
dis-	apart, separate
im-, in-, ir-	not

Stems	Meanings
acro	high (place)
aero	air
agora	marketplace, gathering place
aqua, hydro	water
onym	name
orexi	appetite, hunger
phobia	fear
psych	mind
therap	treatment
xeno	foreign, strange

1. _____ hydrophobia
2. _____ abnormal
3. _____ xenophobia
4. _____ antisocial
5. _____ anonymous
6. _____ agoraphobia
7. _____ dissociate
8. _____ psychotherapy
9. _____ acrophobia
10. _____ anorexia

a. angry or harmful toward society
b. having or giving no name; of unknown or unnamed origin
c. fear of being out in crowded, public places
d. treatment of mental problems
e. without wanting to eat (a psychological disorder)
f. not normal
g. to separate from others
h. fear or hatred of strangers, foreigners, or anything strange
i. fear of high places
j. fear of water

.∴⋮⋮⋮ **Part Three** Reading in the Academic World

Before Reading

A. Vocabulary Preparation.   The following textbook selection contains words that will be new to you. Guess the meaning of some of these from the contexts that follow. When you write your guess, be sure to use the same part of speech as that of the underlined word. After you guess the meaning, check with a dictionary to see if your guess was close.

1. I had a sudden <u>impulse</u> to run out of the room, but I stopped myself from doing this.

My Guess: _____

Dictionary Definition: _____

2. His <u>motive</u> for robbing the store was to get money to buy drugs.

My Guess: _____

Dictionary Definition: _____

3. He hopes to <u>overcome</u> his fear of flying so that he can begin to travel again.

My Guess: _____

Dictionary Definition: _____

4. I know that my fear is <u>irrational</u>; I can't explain it logically, but it's very real to me.

My Guess: _____

Dictionary Definition: _____

5. Applying to a university can be a lengthy <u>procedure</u>. There are many steps to go through.

My Guess: _____

Dictionary Definition: _____

B. Thinking Ahead.   The following selection presents four (of the many) types of therapy for people with psychological disorders. What do you expect to read about? In other words, what kinds of psychotherapy do you already know about?

Reading

As you read the following textbook selection, mark any phrases or sentences that answer this question and lead you to the main ideas.

• What happens in each type of therapy?

Approaches to Psychological Therapy

For a long time **psychoanalysis** was the only formalized psychotherapy practiced in Western society. It was this type of therapy that gave rise to the classic
5 picture of a bearded Viennese doctor seated behind a patient who is lying on a couch. Psychoanalysis is based on the theories of Sigmund Freud. According to Freud's views, psychological disturbances are due to anxi-
10 ety about hidden conflicts in the unconscious parts of one's personality. One job of the psychoanalyst, therefore, is to help make the patients aware of the unconscious impulses, desires, and fears that are causing the
15 anxiety. Psychoanalysts believe that if patients can understand their unconscious motives, they have taken the first step toward gaining control over their behavior and freeing themselves of their problems.
20 Such understanding is called **insight.**

Psychoanalysis is a slow procedure. It may take years of fifty-minute sessions several times a week before the patient is able to make fundamental changes in her life.
25 Throughout this time, the analyst assists his patient in a complete examination of the unconscious motives behind her behavior. This task begins with the analyst telling the patient to relax and talk about everything
30 that comes into her mind. This method is called **free association.**

As the patient lies on the couch, she may describe her dreams, discuss private thoughts, or recall long-forgotten experi-
35 ences. The psychoanalyst often says nothing for long periods of time. The psychoanalyst also occasionally makes remarks or asks questions that guide the patient, or he may suggest an unconscious motive or factor that
40 explains something the patient has been talking about, but most of the work is done by the patient herself.

Psychoanalysis has sometimes been criticized for being "all talk and no action."
45 In **behavior therapy** there is much more emphasis on action. Rather than spending a large amount of time going into the patient's past history or the details of his or her dreams, the behavior therapist concentrates
50 on finding out what is specifically wrong with the patient's current life and takes steps to change it.

The idea behind behavior therapy is that a disturbed person is one who has *learned* to
55 behave in the wrong way. The therapist's job, therefore, is to "reeducate" the patient. The reasons for the patient's undesirable behavior are not important; what is important is to change the behavior. To bring about such
60 changes, the therapist uses certain conditioning techniques first discovered in animal laboratories.

One technique used by behavior therapists is **systematic desensitization.** This
65 method is used to overcome irrational fears and anxieties the patient has learned (Smith,

1990). The goal of desensitization therapy is to encourage people to imagine the feared situation while relaxing. For example, suppose a student is terrified of speaking in front of large groups—that, in fact, his fear makes him unable to speak when called on in class. How would desensitization therapy change this person's behavior?

The therapist might have the student make a list of all the aspects of talking to others that he finds frightening. Perhaps the most frightening aspect is actually standing before an audience, and the least frightening is speaking to a single other person. The client lists his fears, from the most frightening on down. Then the therapist begins teaching the patient to relax. When he knows how to relax completely, the client is ready for the next step. The client tries to imagine as clearly as possible the least disturbing scene on his list. As he thinks about speaking to a single stranger, the student may feel a mild anxiety. But because the therapist has taught him how to relax, the patient learns to think about the experience without being afraid. The therapist attempts to replace anxiety with its opposite, relaxation. The procedure is followed step by step through the list of anxiety-arousing events.

In the forms of therapy described thus far, the troubled person is usually alone with the therapist. In **group therapy,** however, she is in the company of others. There are several advantages to this situation. Group therapy gives the troubled person practical experience with one of her biggest problems—getting along with other people. A person in group therapy also has a chance to see how other people are struggling with problems similar to her own, and she discovers what other people think of her. She,

in turn, can express what she thinks of them, and in this exchange she discovers where she is mistaken in her views of herself and of other people and where she is correct (Drum, 1990).

Another advantage to group therapy is the fact that one therapist can help a large number of people. Most group therapy sessions are led by a trained therapist who makes suggestions, clarifies points, and keeps activities from getting out of control. In this way, her training and experience are used to help as many as 20 people at once, although 8–10 is a more comfortable number.

Therapists often suggest, after talking to a patient, that the entire family should work at group therapy. This method is particularly useful because the members of the group are all people of great importance in one another's lives. In family therapy it is possible to work on the complicated relationships that have led one or more members in the family to experience emotional suffering.

An increasing number of self-help groups have emerged in recent years. These voluntary groups, composed of people who share a particular problem, are often conducted without a professional therapist. During regularly scheduled meetings, members of the group come together to discuss their difficulties and to provide support and possible solutions. Self-help groups have been formed to deal with problems ranging from alcoholism, overeating, and drug addiction, to child abuse, widowhood, single parenting, adjusting to cancer, and gambling. The best known self-help group is Alcoholics Anonymous (AA), which was founded in 1935. Far more people find treatment for their drinking problems

through AA than in psychotherapy or
150 treatment centers.

The various "talking" and "learning" therapies described so far have been
aimed primarily at patients who are still
generally capable of functioning within
155 society. But what of those people who are
not capable of clear thinking or who are
dangerous to themselves or others? **Antipsychotic drug therapy** is used in the
treatment of schizophrenia. The most
160 popular of these medicines have been the
phenothiazines—including Thorazine
and Stelazine. Patients with schizophrenia who take these medications improve
in a number of ways: they become less
165 withdrawn, become less confused, have
fewer auditory hallucinations, and are
less irritable. Although the patient who
takes antipsychotic drugs is often im-
proved enough to leave the hospital, he
170 or she may have trouble adjusting to the
outside world. Many patients now face
the "revolving door" syndrome of going
to a mental hospital, being released, re-
turning to the hospital, being released
175 again, and so on. Phenothiazines also
have a number of unpleasant side effects,
including a dry mouth, blurred vision,
sleepiness, and muscle disorders.

Another class of drugs, called *antide-*
180 *pressants*, relieve depression. Interestingly, they do not affect the mood of
nondepressed people. It is almost as if
these medicines supply a chemical that
some depressed people don't naturally
185 have. Some of the antidepressants have
severe side effects. However, Prozac was
introduced in 1987 and is typically much
safer than other antidepressants.

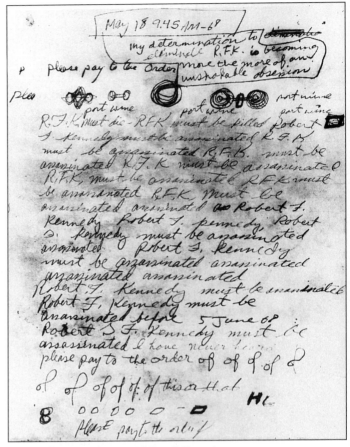

From the diary of the killer of Robert F. Kennedy,
this page shows the thought disturbances that
are characteristic of schizophrenia.

Source: "Approaches to Psychological Therapy" adapted from Richard A. Kasschau, *Understanding Psychology*, pp. 397–398 and 405–410.
Copyright © 1995 by Glencoe Publishing Company. Reprinted with the permission of the publishers.

After Reading

A. Main Ideas.   Look over your markings for information that explains each kind of therapy. (For some therapies you've probably marked a lot. For others you haven't marked as much.) Compare your markings with those of another student. Do you agree about what is important?

B. Comprehension Check: Making Inferences.   The author clearly *states* some information directly and *implies* (suggests) other ideas. Look back at the selection to answer these questions.

1. What do you think the author believes about psychoanalysis?

2. Which therapy might the author suggest for

- a phobia?
- schizophrenia?
- alcoholism?
- depression?

3. What might be the most expensive therapy? The least expensive? Why?

C. Application.   What might be the problem of the patient in the cartoon? What kind of therapy do you think he is going through?

Ziggy

D. Finding Important Details.   Go back to the reading and mark—in a different color—the advantages and disadvantages of each therapy. Then put these on the chart that follows. Some of these are just implied, so they might be harder to find than those that are stated.

Therapy	Advantages	Disadvantages

Compare your answers with another student's. Were there any kinds of therapy that didn't have any advantages (or disadvantages)?

E. Discussion.   With a partner, discuss this question: If you needed help, which type of therapy would you feel most comfortable with? Why?

⠂⠒⠒⠒ **Part Four** The Mechanics of Writing

In Part Five you are going to write a paragraph about one method of psychological therapy. To write this, you will need to use correct sentence structures to express advantages and disadvantages. In addition, you may need to use the passive voice and relative clauses. Part Four will help you with this.

Understanding and Using the Passive Voice

You will notice a lot of passive voice in the three reading passages in this chapter.

Example: Psychiatrists interviewed the man from the Ozarks. (active voice)

   The man from the Ozarks was interviewed by psychiatrists. (passive voice)

We use the passive voice in this way (with *by* or another preposition) to emphasize the object (from the active voice) and the verb.

- In the preceding example, we use the passive voice if it is more important to know *whom* the psychiatrists interviewed than *who* interviewed the man.
- As you saw in Chapter Two, we don't use the *by* phrase at all if the subject (from the active voice) is *obvious, unnecessary,* or *unknown.*

Examples: The man *was arrested.* (It's obvious that he was arrested by the police.)

   He *was hospitalized* for mental illness. (It's unnecessary to say that he was hospitalized by psychiatrists.)

   If he had stayed home, he *would have been considered* to be perfectly normal. (We don't know *who* would have considered him normal—probably people in general in his hometown.)

The passive voice consists of the *be* verb and the past participle of another verb. The *be* verb can be in any tense except present perfect continuous or past perfect continuous, or it can have a modal.

Examples: is done   will be done

   was done   might be done

   has been done   should be done

   is being done   would have been done

A. Using the Passive Voice.   Change these active voice sentences to the passive voice. Use the same tense as in the active voice. In most cases, you won't need a *by* phrase.

1. Psychiatrists classify phobias as simple phobias, social phobias, and agoraphobia.

   _____

   _____

2. We find just four disorders in all cultures of the world.

   _____

   _____

3. According to the belief, either demons or gods possessed that person.

   _____

   _____

4. Cultural factors may influence the specific symptoms of the disorder.

   _____

   _____

5. A violent outburst characterizes "amok," a behavior that we find in Malaysia. (Note: Change both clauses.)

   _____

   _____

6. People have criticized psychoanalysis for being "all talk and no action."

   _____

   _____

7. A trained therapist leads group therapy sessions.

   _____

   _____

8. People have formed self-help groups to deal with problems such as alcoholism.

   _____

   _____

Review of Adjective Clauses (Relative Clauses) in Definitions

As you saw in Chapter One, a definition often includes an adjective clause.

Examples: A manic-depressive is a person <u>*who* suffers from bipolar disorder</u>.

Schizophrenia is a serious disorder <u>*in which* people lose touch with reality and have hallucinations</u>.

B. Writing Definitions with Relative Clauses. Define each word or expression below in a complete sentence. Use a relative clause beginning with *who* or *in which* in each. Look back at the readings if necessary.

1. anorexia nervosa

_____

_____

2. a schizophrenic

_____

_____

3. *amok*

_____

_____

4. a psychologist

_____

_____

5. *kitsunetsuki*

_____

_____

Writing about Advantages and Disadvantages

When you write about advantages (good points) and disadvantages or drawbacks (bad points), it helps to know the following structures.

| a(n) one another | + | advantage disadvantage drawback | of to | noun noun phrase gerund | be | noun noun phrase (the fact) that + clause |

Examples: One advantage to psychoanalysis is that people can become aware of the causes of their disorder.

A disadvantage of going through psychoanalysis is the fact that it can take many years of sessions.

Another (implicit) drawback is the expense.

C. Practice. Choose two topics from the following list. Write three sentences about the advantages and/or disadvantages of *each* of these two topics.

- a new car
- beginning college in middle age
- learning a new language
- watching TV
- living in another country
- marriage
- having a phobia (hydrophobia, acrophobia, agoraphobia, etc.)

Using Adverbial Conjunctions of Addition and Contradiction

In Chapter Two you learned how to use adverbial conjunctions. Here is a brief review of two groups of these transitional words that are common in academic writing.

in addition
moreover $\Big\} = and$
however
on the other hand $\Big\} = but$

Examples: One advantage to psychoanalysis is that people can become aware of the causes of their disorder. <u>However,</u> a disadvantage of going through analysis is the fact that it can take many years of sessions; <u>in addition,</u> an implicit drawback is the expense.

Use: Adverbial conjunctions often begin a sentence or independent clause. There is a period or semicolon before the adverbial conjunction. There is a comma after it.

D. Sentence Combining: Adverbial Conjunctions. Combine each pair of sentences with *in addition, moreover, however,* or *on the other hand.*

1. A person who hears voices of the deceased may be considered to be disturbed.

In Plains Indian culture this isn't seen as a disturbance at all.

_____

_____

2. People who are agoraphobic usually stop going to movies or crowded stores.

Some will not leave their homes at all.

_____

_____

3. Catatonic schizophrenia is rare in North America and western Europe.

In India, 80 percent of those with schizophrenia are catatonic.

_____

_____

4. All of us are sometimes depressed, and there is nothing abnormal about this.

In some people, the depression is intense and possibly dangerous.

_____

_____

5. People with schizophrenia experience hallucinations and delusions.

They may be unable to focus their attention.

_____

_____

E. Sentence Combining: Writing Paragraphs. Combine your sentences in Exercise C to form two short paragraphs. Use *in addition, moreover, however,* and *on the other hand.*

Note: Be sure not to *over*use adverbial conjunctions. In a paragraph in which you list a number of advantages and disadvantages, it would be poor style to begin every sentence or independent clause with an adverbial conjunction.

Part Five Writing in the Academic World

Before Writing

writing Strategy

Paraphrasing and Summarizing

Two of the most important skills that you'll need in writing academic English are paraphrasing and summarizing.

When you write a *paraphrase,* you restate information *in different words,* without changing the author's meaning at all. A *summary* is similar to a paraphrase, but in a summary you both paraphrase and *shorten* the original text.

Paraphrasing

When you write a paraphrase

DO	DO NOT
• change words to their synonyms	• use quotation marks
• change passive to active	• include your own opinion
• change active to passive	• change words that have no synonyms
• use different conjunctions with the same meaning	• change specialized or technical vocabulary
• change sentence structure	
• cite your source (*see the following*)	

Citing Your Source

When you use the words *or ideas* of another person in a paragraph or essay, you MUST cite your source (give credit to that person and say where you found the information). If you don't cite your source, you are *plagiarizing*—i.e., stealing. Here are some of the many ways to cite your source:

According to Joe Blow in *Health,* . . . .

Josephina Blow, in her book *New Horizons in Health,* points out that. . . .

In *Health,* Joe Blow tells us that. . . .

In her article, "Depression and Medication" in *Psychology Today,* Josephina Blow states that . . .

Combining Sentences in Paraphrasing

In paraphrasing, you might also combine several short sentences into one—again, without changing the meaning of the original text.

Here is one way to paraphrase the following two sentences, but there are certainly other possible ways.

Example: ORIGINAL: "No human can go through life without being depressed. For people with major depressive disorder, the bouts of depression are extended and interfere with their ability to function in daily life" (Blow, *Health*).

PARAPHRASE: As Joe Blow points out in *Health,* all humans are depressed from time to time; however, people with major depressive disorder suffer from long periods of depression that hamper their efforts to go about everyday activities.

A. Practice.   Paraphrase these sentences. Be sure to cite your source. (All of these sentences were written by Richard A. Kasschau in a book called *Understanding Psychology.*)

1. It is often difficult to draw a line between normal and abnormal behavior.

_____

_____

2. The fact that it is difficult to define abnormality does not mean that no such thing exists.

_____

_____

3. We should be very cautious about judging a person to be "mentally ill" just because he or she acts in a way that we cannot understand.

_____

_____

4. People with anxiety-based disorders are deeply anxious and seem unable to free themselves of worries and fears.

_____

_____

5. Their emotions hamper their ability to function effectively. In extreme cases, a mood may cause individuals to lose touch with reality or seriously threaten their health or lives.

_____

_____

 writing Strategy

Summarizing

When you write a *summary,* you use all of the same techniques that you use in paraphrasing, but a summary is *shorter.* In a summary, include only the main idea(s) and most important details. You might summarize one paragraph in a single sentence, for example, or summarize a whole book in a few pages. You will often have to *summarize* in academic writing.

In writing a summary you should remember several points.

- Understand the material well before writing your summary.

- Use your own words; e.g., use synonyms, different word forms, different grammatical structures, and different transition words.

- Don't add your own opinion.

- Cite your source (author and title) in the first sentence of the summary.

HINT: It is often a terrible temptation to copy phrases from the original. To avoid the temptation of copying, try these steps:

- Make sure that you read the material several times and understand it very well before beginning your summary.

- Turn the original material upside down or put it away. Do not look at the original as you write your summary.

You will frequently have to summarize on essay exams, on which you *can't* look at the original.

Example: Here is a summary of three paragraphs on pages 164–165 of this chapter:

> In *Understanding Psychology,* Richard A. Kasschau points out that there are three ways to define a person as psychologically abnormal. One is to say that anyone who is different from most other people is abnormal. Another is that an abnormal person cannot get along in everyday life. The third implies that an abnormal person is not psychologically healthy or functioning at some ideal level. However, Kasschau cautions that we ought to be careful before we label someone as "mentally ill."

B. Practice.   Summarize the paragraph about anorexia nervosa on page 169 of this chapter. Then compare your summary with 1) the original and 2) your classmates' summaries.

C. Planning Your Paragraph.

1. Look over the main ideas that you marked on pages 174–176. Make sure that you understand each approach to therapy very well. Take brief notes. Then close your book and write a short summary of *each* of these approaches: **behavior therapy, group therapy,** and **drug therapy.**

2. Look over the advantages and disadvantages to each approach that you noted on the chart on page 178. Is there one approach for which you have more information than the others?

D. Choosing a Topic.   In a writing assignment or on an essay exam, you may be given a limited choice of topic. It's important for you to choose the topic that you understand the best and about which you have enough—but not *too* much—to say. For the writing assignment in this chapter, choose one of the three approaches to therapy from the preceding exercise (C):

- behavior therapy
- group therapy
- drug therapy

This should be the approach for which you have the clearest summary and several clear advantages (and/or disadvantages).

Writing

Writing Assignment: First Draft.   Write one paragraph about the approach to therapy that you've chosen. In the first few sentences, summarize this approach. Then in the rest of the paragraph, present the advantages and/or disadvantages to this approach. (Use your chart on page 178 to help you with this information.) Write complete sentences about the advantages and disadvantages; be sure to use the structures on page 182. As an example, here is a summary of psychoanalysis from page 174, including the advantages and disadvantages.

Example: According to Richard A. Kasschau in *Understanding Psychology*, the theories of Sigmund Freud form the basis of psychotherapy. Freud believed that psychological problems are the result of conflicts in a person's unconscious. The psychoanalyst's task is to guide the patient through perhaps several years of sessions in which the patient explores the unconscious motives for her behavior and becomes aware of the causes of her anxiety. One advantage of psychotherapy is that the patient can gain insight. However, a clear disadvantage is the lengthy process. Another implied drawback is that because the process takes so many years, it is most certainly expensive.

After Writing

A. Self-Check.   Read over your paragraph and answer the questions on the following checklist. Write yes or no.

B. Classmate's Check.   Exchange papers with a classmate and check each other's paragraphs. Write yes or no on your classmate's checklist.

editing Checklist

Points To Check For	My Check	My Classmate's Check
1. Is the source cited in the first sentence?	_____	_____
2. Is the summary in different words from the original text?	_____	_____
3. Was opinion avoided?	_____	_____
4. Are the advantages (or disadvantages) presented with the correct grammatical structure?	_____	_____
5. Are transition words used correctly (and not overused)?	_____	_____
6. If the passive voice is used, is it used correctly?	_____	_____
7. Other: _____	_____	_____

Second Draft.   Use the answers on the checklist to guide you in your revision. Then give your paper to your teacher.

Health

chapter Seven

Medicine and Drugs: Addictive Substances

In this chapter, you'll read about various kinds of addiction and what can be done about this problem. You'll write a persuasive paragraph about a possible solution to drug, alcohol, or tobacco abuse.

Part One   The Babies of Addiction

Before Reading

A. Discussion.   In small groups, answer these questions.

1. If a pregnant woman is addicted to drugs or alcohol, what might happen to her unborn baby?

2. In your country, who takes care of the baby of a mother who cannot take care of her child because of her addiction?

3. In your country, do many people *adopt* a child—in other words, take someone else's child into their home and legally become the child's parents?

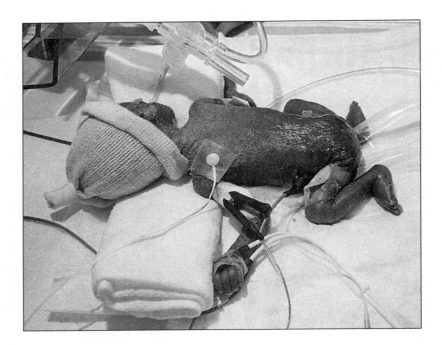

Reading

As you read the following two passages, think about the answer to this question.

• What are some problems of babies born to mothers who smoked crack (an illegal drug; a strong form of cocaine that is smoked) or drank alcohol during pregnancy?

The Babies of Addiction

Arthur was already 3 days old when his aunt found him in the Houston garage where his crack-addicted mother had abandoned him. Arthur's aunt adopted him, but at 13 months, he was so wild that his aunt called him "possessed." She brought him to a special program for infants sponsored by Houston's Mental Health and Mental Retardation authority. There, he would not let his teacher, Geynille Agee, come closer than eight feet before he began hurling toys at her. Two years later Agee thinks she has made a little progress with the boy; he can now walk calmly down the hall holding his aunt's hand—something he could never do before.

The first wave of crack babies is just approaching school age, and educators are frustrated and bewildered by their behavior. "They operate only on an instinctual level," says Agee of her students. "They eat and sleep, eat and sleep. Something has been left out." Sometimes withdrawn, these children may have trouble playing or even talking with other kids. Some have tremors or periods when they seem to tune out the world. No one yet knows how to undo the damage caused by a pregnant woman's drug use.

Source: "The Babies of Addiction: Crack and Alcohol" from Barbara Kantrowitz, "The Crack Children," from *Newsweek* (February 12, 1990): 62. Copyright © 1990 by Newsweek, Inc. Reprinted with the permission of *Newsweek*. All rights reserved.

When I adopted Abel in 1971, I was informed that his birth mother was alcoholic, but at the time not even the medical community was aware of the potential consequences when a woman drank—even moderately—during pregnancy. Now, sadly, I knew better. Fetal alcohol syndrome [FAS] could be manifested in a variety of symptoms ranging from the physical (heart, hearing and vision problems, neurological impairments, deformation of the brain) to learning deficits affecting abstract thinking and consistent with low I.Q. My son, to one degree or another, had them all.

There is no real cure for the more than 10,000 FAS-afflicted babies born annually in the United States. A majority are Caucasian, but in some Native American groups, like the one from which I adopted Abel, nearly 25 percent of all infants show some degree of damage from maternal alcohol use.

Especially during Abel's childhood, before the full magnitude of his learning block was undeniable, I indulged in the persistent fantasy of his brain as a kind of messy room. If I could somehow get inside his head, straighten up the clutter, turn on the lights, suddenly he would become normal. But the door stayed firmly locked. Finally I gave up, let Abel rest. For me, it was defeat. For him, I'm sure it was a great relief.

Source: "My Son's Devotion Was Total," (excerpt) by Michael Dorris, from *New Choices for Retirement Living* (December 1993–January 1994): 28. Copyright © 1993 by Michael Dorris. Reprinted with the permission of Rembar & Curtis.

After Reading

A. Main Ideas. Work with a partner to find symptoms (in the two passages) of children whose mothers smoked crack or drank alcohol during pregnancy. Write them in the blanks.

Crack	Alcohol
_____	_____
_____	_____
_____	_____
_____	_____

reading Strategy

Understanding Metaphors

A metaphor is a phrase that describes one thing by comparing it to something else.

Examples: His round moon face shone with pleasure.

Her heart, a cold tomb, would not open for anyone.

B. Finding Metaphors. What metaphor does Michael Dorris use in this passage about his son Abel?

C. Extension. In small groups, discuss this question: What are some problems for a society that has many babies born to addicted mothers?

D. Response Writing. Choose *one* of the following questions to answer.

- Should crack or FAS babies be taken away from their mothers? Why or why not?

- What should society do about women who use drugs or alcohol during pregnancy?

- What should be the responsibility of the fathers of these babies?

For ten minutes, write as much as you can in answering the question you chose. Don't stop writing to use a dictionary or to worry about grammar.

Did You Know?

■ Each year in the U.S. between 5,000 and 10,000 children are born with fetal alcohol syndrome.

■ Up to 100,000 children may be born with fetal alcohol effects, which are less severe than FAS but are still serious results of drinking alcohol during pregnancy.

■ Exposure of a fetus to alcohol is now a leading cause of mental retardation in the United States.

Source: *Health, A Guide to Wellness*, p. 498, by Mary Bronson Merki and Don Merki. Glencoe/McGraw-Hill, New York, 1994.

. : : : : Part Two Addiction in Developing Countries

Before Reading

A. Vocabulary Preparation.   The following passage has some words that will be new to you. What can you guess about each underlined word that follows? Write your guess on each line. Then compare your answers with another student's.

1. There are thousands of babies born to addicted mothers, and these babies will suffer from physical and mental problems for the rest of their lives. This is a truly <u>disastrous</u> situation.

   My Guess: _____

2. I felt a sharp <u>pang</u> of hunger in my stomach and realized that I hadn't eaten all day.

   My Guess: _____

3. My daughter loves ice cream and other sweets. I hate to <u>deny</u> her the pleasure of eating them, but on the other hand, I really don't want her to eat something that's not good for her health.

   My Guess: _____

4. The <u>consumption</u> of alcohol is high in some countries, but in Islamic countries it is quite low. In some countries there is a high consumption of meat while in others people eat very little meat.

   My Guess: _____

5. He's addicted to marijuana, heroin, cocaine, and other <u>illicit</u> drugs.

   My Guess: _____

6. Magazine ads <u>link</u> alcohol with the idea of freedom, excitement, and fun.

My Guess: _____

7. I broke this cup, and I don't want to throw it away. I just need a little <u>glue</u> so that I can put it back together.

My Guess: _____

8. The cat carefully <u>sniffed</u> at the bit of food. When she decided that it smelled good, she quickly ate it.

My Guess: _____

B. Thinking Ahead.   You know that some people are addicted to drugs or alcohol. What other addictions do people have?

C. Making Predictions.   The reading passage discusses several addictive substances in some developing countries. In your opinion, why might people develop an addiction?

Reading

As you read the passage, mark with a felt-tip pen the answers to these questions.

1. Why do people use—and abuse—tobacco, alcohol, and glue?

2. Why do indigenous people value psychoactive substances?

Addiction in Developing Countries

A recent edition of *World Health*, the magazine of the World Health Organization, describes the disastrous effect of various addictions—to tobacco, alcohol, glue, and
5 drugs—in different parts of the world.

Tobacco Use

Smoking—the cause of about three million deaths every year—is especially risky in poor countries. Very poor people often use tobacco as an appetite suppressant—a cheap
10 way to stop the pangs of hunger. Among people who already have anemia because of lack of iron in their diet, the tobacco further reduces the ability of the blood to carry oxygen. However, governments in developing
15 countries don't often make decisions that might deny poor people the small pleasure of smoking or chewing tobacco. In India, for example, approximately half of all adults and 10% of all children are dependent on
20 tobacco, [and] the cigarette industry has reason to believe it can soon increase cigarette production by 60%.

Alcohol in Russia

The consumption of alcohol in the former Soviet Union was traditionally high. The
25 true amount was usually higher than the official sales figures due to the production of *samogen,* illicit homemade alcohol. Today in Russia, it is still difficult to know for certain how many people are dependent on alcohol;
30 the real total may be as high as seven to eight million, and this number is rising. Government efforts to control alcohol are associated with the previous, communist system and are not popular. In recent years, European
35 and American brands of alcohol have become symbols of Western lifestyles, and advertising is linking the drinking of alcohol with freedom and social success, which seem attractive to many people.

Addiction Among Street Children

40 The combination of rapid growth of cities and lack of economic growth has led to an increasing problem in much of the developing world: street children, many of them

homeless. Children as young as eight or even
45 six can be found using psychoactive substances—that is, substances that change the normal functioning of the brain. In all parts of the developing world, glue is the substance which is most abused. It is cheap,
50 available, and provides a "rapid high" when children sniff it from the container or from a plastic bag. In time, children may add marijuana, alcohol, cigarettes, and other substances such as cocaine.

Substance Abuse Among Indigenous Peoples

55 There are an estimated 300 million indigenous people worldwide who are living on their traditional lands in over 70 countries. They are called indigenous peoples because they were living on their lands before set-
60 tlers came from other countries. They have a great cultural, ethnic, linguistic, and religious diversity; some are hunters and gatherers living in rainforests, and others are business leaders in the world's financial
65 centers.

Nevertheless, most indigenous groups share a common heritage in their use of psychoactive substances. Traditionally, they highly value these natural substances, found
70 in the local environment, for their medicinal and nutritional qualities and for their use in religious practices. Among Native Americans, hallucinogens (including certain types of mushrooms and peyote) have been widely
75 used to help people communicate with the spirit world. In Asia, opium has a long history of use for relaxation and as a medicine to relieve pain. In Africa, the use of hashish

An Australian poster warns indigenous communities about the risk of alcohol.

and *khat* (leaves that are chewed or made
80 into a drink) forms part of the lives of some
indigenous people.

Within these cultures, strict traditional taboos and laws have helped to regulate the use of these psychoactive substances. How-
85 ever, many of these cultures have eroded as global development occurs, and the people have been exposed to "outside" attitudes and beliefs. In the case of alcohol, there is no tradition of use and social control among
90 many indigenous groups, so its introduction into certain communities (Australian Aborigines, North American Indians, etc.) was a disaster. A change from opium-smoking to opium-and-heroin-injecting
95 among the hill tribes of Southeast Asia has been a major factor in the spread of AIDS in those communities.

What Can Be Done?

The methods to help addicted people in developed countries might not be effective in
100 all cultures. The World Health Organization (WHO) has recommendations for specific programs. To help addicted street children, for example, WHO recommends a three-step program. In the first step, a new type of pro-
105 fessional called a street educator makes contact with street children, becomes their friend, gives them counseling, and helps them to establish trust in the adult world. This step may take six to nine months or
110 more. In the second step, the children go to a diagnostic center where their physical, psychological, and social problems will be studied, and a treatment plan will be established. This may take a week. Then the chil-
115 dren go to a center for psycho-social and medical treatment, which might take nine months or more. It is important to have such education and counseling programs because all the indications are that the numbers of
120 street children will increase in the future.

Source: *World Health*, 48, no. 4, July–August 1995.

After Reading

A. Main Ideas.   Look back at the sentences that you marked to help you find answers to these questions. Then compare your answers with a partner's.

1. What is one reason that people in poor countries smoke or chew tobacco?

2. Why are European and American brands of alcohol popular in Russia?

3. Why do some street children sniff glue?

4. Why do indigenous people traditionally value psychoactive substances?

B. Comprehension Check: Details.   With a partner, answer these questions.

1. What are some examples of psychoactive substances?

2. Why was the *traditional* use of psychoactive substances not such a problem in indigenous cultures?

3. What are two examples of serious problems that occur when indigenous people have been exposed to attitudes and beliefs outside their culture?

C. Vocabulary Check.   Find a word or expression in the passage for each definition that follows. The numbers in parentheses refer to lines.

1. a way to stop the pangs of hunger (5–10): _____

2. a condition in which there is a lack of iron in the body (10–15): _____

3. people who were living on their lands before settlers came from other countries (55–60): _____

4. traditional rules or restrictions (80–85): _____

5. taking into the body with a needle (90–95): _____

6. a center where people discover what a problem is (110–115): _____

D. Understanding Italics.   There are two words in italics in the passage (in addition to the name of a magazine). Find them quickly.

1. Why are they in italics?

2. What do these two words mean?

E. Reference.   What does the pronoun or possessive adjective mean in each context that follows? Write the meaning on the line.

1. The cigarette industry has reason to believe <u>it</u> can soon increase cigarette production by 60%.

   it = _____

2. Glue is the substance which is most abused. <u>It</u> is cheap, available, and provides a "rapid high."

   it = _____

3. There are an estimated 300 million indigenous people worldwide who are living on <u>their</u> traditional lands.

   their = _____

4. Most indigenous groups share a common heritage in <u>their</u> use of psychoactive substances.

   their = _____

5. In the case of alcohol, there is no tradition of use and social control among many indigenous groups, so <u>its</u> introduction into certain communities was a disaster.

   its = _____

6. A street educator makes contact with street children, gives <u>them</u> counseling, and helps <u>them</u> to establish trust in the adult world.

   them = _____

F. Vocabulary Expansion.   Use a dictionary to help you find other parts of speech of these words.

Noun	Verb	Adjective
1. disaster	X	_____
2. consumption	_____	_____
3. _____	deny	X
4. diversity	_____	_____
5. _____	erode	X
6. hallucination	_____	_____

G. Discussion. In small groups, discuss these questions.

1. What substances do people use (or abuse) in your culture? What reasons can you give for this use (or abuse)?

2. Are there any government programs to help people with addictions?

3. Are there advertisements for cigarettes or alcohol in magazines in your country? Are there commercials (ads) on TV for cigarettes or alcohol?

4. In your country, are there ads *against* the use of tobacco, alcohol, or drugs?

H. Critical Thinking. In small groups, write a short radio commercial and design a poster to persuade children not to start 1) smoking, 2) drinking alcohol, 3) sniffing glue, or 4) using drugs. (Choose just *one* of the four.) Before you begin to write, consider these questions:

• Why might children be attracted to these substances?

• What arguments might children truly pay attention to?

. : : : : : **Part Three** Reading in the Academic World

Before Reading

A. Vocabulary Preparation. The following textbook passage has some words that may be new to you. What can you guess about each underlined word that follows? Write your guess on each line and compare your answers with another student's.

1. When she was pregnant, she <u>craved</u> strange foods. Once, her husband had to drive to the store at midnight because she had such a strong desire for chocolate ice cream and pickles.

   My Guess: _____

2. It's really hard to <u>cope with</u> him when he's been drinking. I wish he would stay away from alcohol so that we wouldn't have to deal with this problem any longer.

   My Guess: _____

3. You can <u>rely on</u> her to help you. We've depended on her for many years because she's such a responsible person.

   My Guess: _____

4. When he's <u>sober</u>, he's a wonderful person, but when he's drunk, he changes completely and becomes a kind of monster.

My Guess: _____

5. This is <u>confidential</u> information, so please don't tell anyone.

My Guess: _____

B. Thinking Ahead.   The textbook passage explains what addiction is and what can be done to help addicts. Before you read, look at the chart *Addiction: The Downward Slide* and discuss it with a partner.

1. Do you think it is possible for people to remain at Step 1 and not move on to the other steps?

2. Can you think of famous people in the news who seem to be at Step 6?

3. In your opinion, what can friends or family of an addict do to prevent this person from "hitting bottom"— reaching Step 6?

4. What is life like for the family of a person at Step 4, 5, or 6?

Source: "Addiction: The Downward Slide" from Mary Bronson Merki and Don Merki, *Health: A Guide to Wellness.* Copyright © 1994 by Glencoe/ McGraw-Hill. Reprinted with the permission of the publishers.

ADDICTION: THE DOWNWARD SLIDE

These steps show the way an addiction to alcohol or other drugs might develop.

Step 1: First use/occasional use
- Takes first drink or uses other drug for the first time
- Likes the way it feels and reduces stress
- Uses the drug in social settings

Step 2: Occasional trouble with drug
- Shows mood swings or personality changes (may happen on the first use)
- Has greater tolerance than others—for example, can outdrink others without seeming drunk
- May cry, get violent, or show high-risk behaviors while drinking and using drugs
- May have blackouts, not remembering what was said or done

Step 3: Regular use of drug
- Finds that tolerance increases—needs more of a drug and may crave it more frequently
- Tries to control drug use but cannot
- Feels guilty after binges, or episodes
- Hangs out with others who drink or use drugs
- Denies problem; gets angry when others suggest a drinking or drug use problem

Step 4: Multiple drug use
- May combine or switch drugs for new and stronger effects or to assure supply
- May become cross-addicted, or hooked on more than one kind of drug

Step 5: Increasing dependency
- Needs drug just to function
- Finds that drug no longer has same effect; needs drug just to stop shaking or feeling sick
- Loses interest in family, friends, school, job, sports—everything but drugs

Step 6: Total dependency
- Suffers major loss because of addiction, such as getting thrown out of school, losing a relationship, causing a car crash, being hospitalized, getting arrested
- Feels physically and emotionally defeated

Reading

As you read the textbook passage, think about the answers to these questions.

1. What is addiction?

2. What are helpful or harmful things that the family of an addict can do?

Addiction: What Can Be Done about It?

An addiction is a physiological or psychological dependence on a substance or activity. One can be addicted to alcohol, drugs, tobacco, gambling—even food. In this passage we will discuss addiction to

5 alcohol and other drugs. Physiological dependence means that the body has become accustomed to a drug and needs these chemicals just to function. The body of an addict craves these substances. Physiological dependence is determined when a person

10 experiences tolerance and withdrawal. Tolerance means that the body becomes used to the effect of the drug. The body then requires larger doses of the drug

> **Did You Know?**
>
> According to *Prevention's Book of Health Facts:*
>
> ■ Just one cigarette causes "cigarette breath."
>
> ■ About 75% of deaths from lung cancer among women are caused by smoking.
>
> ■ On average, a cigarette smoker is 10 to 15 times more likely to get lung cancer than a nonsmoker.

to produce the same effect. Withdrawal occurs when the person stops taking a drug on which he or she is physiologically dependent and experiences painful physical symptoms.

15 Psychological dependence means that a person comes to depend on the feeling received from a drug. Psychological dependence often involves denial, in which the addict does not admit or does not realize that he or she is in trouble with alcohol or other drugs. The person believes that he or she can control the use of the drug and is not causing any harm.

Intervention

To "wake up" an addicted person from this state of denial, many families rely on a process

20 called intervention. Intervention means interrupting the downward slide before the addict hits bottom. The process begins with meetings of family members and other people important in the life of the addicted person. They usually meet first with a drug and alcohol counselor and someone from a support group such as Alcoholics Anonymous to learn about addiction and discuss how they have been affected by it. Then they have the actual

25 intervention—a surprise meeting with the addict to
force this person to see how unmanageable his or her
life has become because of the addiction. At this
meeting they present a plan for immediate treatment
and let the addict know that it's time to face the con-
30 sequences of the addiction.

Recovery

Like addiction, recovery—learning to live without
alcohol or drugs—is a process that happens over
time. The first steps are 1) to recognize that there is
a problem with alcohol or drugs and 2) to make the
35 decision to give them up. The third step is to actually
remove these drugs from the body. This process is
called detoxification and should take place under
medical supervision.

People in recovery describe themselves as "re-
40 covering" instead of "recovered." This is because the
recovery process is ongoing and lifelong. Alcoholism and drug dependence cannot be cured. They can,
however, be prevented from progressing further. And
people can begin the recovery process at any point
45 on the downward slide into addiction—even before
they suffer major losses.

Most experts in the field of addiction recommend total abstinence for the recovering
alcoholic and addict. Total abstinence means not using any mood-altering drugs, including alcohol. Long-term studies show that attempts at controlled drinking and drug use
50 usually fail. Even small amounts of alcohol or other drugs can send an addict back into
addiction. Many people in recovery manage to stay drug-free for the rest of their lives.
Others may have relapses—periodic returns to drinking and drug use. Yet despite how
many times the person relapses, the choice of and chance for recovery are always there.

Treatment Choices

A support group is a group of people who share a common problem and work together
55 to help each other and themselves to cope with and recover from that problem. Regular
attendance at such support groups is the most popular form of ongoing treatment for

---

Alcoholism

Alcoholism, or addiction to
alcohol, is considered a
disease by the American
Medical Association (AMA).
Since 1987 drug dependence,
or drug addiction, has also
been considered a disease by
the AMA. Both of these
diseases are described as
chronic (happening over a
long period), **progressive**
(getting worse over time),
and potentially **fatal**
(possible to die from).

Did You Know?

Addiction to cocaine is
increasing. Among those
addicted in the U.S., some
200,000 are in drug treatment,
55,000 are homeless, and
1,530,000 were arrested in
one recent year.

addictions. Support groups such as Alcoholics Anonymous (AA), Narcotics Anonymous, and Cocaine Anonymous have played a major role in helping people to get and stay free of alcohol and drugs. At meetings, which are held frequently all over the world, members 60 provide support and help each other stay sober. Such meetings are confidential; members can remain anonymous because nobody has to give his or her last name. And the meetings are free.

Alcohol and drug treatment centers offer a wide range of services:

- *Detox units* in some hospitals or treatment centers help an addict through detoxifi- 65 cation—usually three to seven days. Some people go directly from detox to a support group.
- *Inpatient treatment centers* are facilities where a person stays for a month or more.
- *Outpatient treatment centers* allow a person to live at home during the treatment and spend a few hours each day at the center.
70 - *Halfway houses* offer housing, counseling, and support meetings for six months to a year to help people learn coping and living skills so that they can return to society.

Codependency

Some people who live with an alcoholic or drug addict become codependent. They are not addicted, but they suffer from a very damaging emotional and social obsession. 75 Codependents try to protect the addict from facing the consequences of the drug problem. They lie for the addict, lend money, make excuses. Such actions, of course, do not help the addict. They just make it possible for him or her to continue in the addiction—and cause a variety of stress-related disorders for the codependent, ranging from depression and eating disorders to high blood pressure.

Source: "Addiction: What Can Be Done About It?" adapted from Mary Bronson Merki and Don Merki, *Health, A Guide to Wellness*, pp. 497–498 and 500–506. Copyright © 1994 by Glencoe/McGraw-Hill. Reprinted with the permission of the publishers.

After Reading

A. Comprehension Check.   With a partner, discuss the answers to these questions.

1. What is addiction?
2. What do codependents do? Do they help an addict?
3. What can the family of an addict do to help him or her stop the downward slide?
4. What are the first two steps that an addict must take to recover from addiction?

B. Vocabulary Check.   Look back at the passage to find words for these definitions. Numbers in parentheses refer to lines.

1. a condition in which the body needs chemical drugs
   just to function (5–10):   _____

2. a condition in which a person depends on the feeling
   that he or she gets from a drug (15–20):   _____

3. a condition in which the body requires larger amounts
   of a drug to produce the same effect (10–15):   _____

4. a condition in which a person stops taking a drug
   and has painful physical symptoms (10–15):   _____

5. a process of interrupting the downward slide
   before an addict hits bottom (20–25):   _____

6. the process of removing drugs from the body (35–40):   _____

7. periodic returns to drinking or drug use after
   an addict has quit (50–55):   _____

C. Vocabulary Expansion.   Use a dictionary to help you find other parts of speech of these words.

Nouns	Adjectives	Verbs
1. dependence	_____	_____
2. addict (person)	_____	X
addiction (condition)	_____	X
3. _____	_____	tolerate
4. _____	_____	rely
5. recovery	_____	_____
X	_____	X

D. Word Journal.   Go back to the passage. Which words are important for you to remember? Put them in your Word Journal.

E. Discussion.   In small groups, answer these questions.

1. There seems to be a lot of drug and alcohol abuse among jazz musicians, rock musicians, and fashion models. What might be some reasons for this? Can you think of other groups of people who have a high rate of substance abuse?

2. In your culture, are there Alcoholics Anonymous groups? Here are some other support groups to help addicted people. Do any of these exist in your country?

> - Al-Anon Family Groups
> - Families Anonymous
> - Gamblers Anonymous
> - Narcotics Anonymous
> - Overeaters Anonymous
> - Parents Anonymous
> - Smokers Anonymous

3. What do people in your culture usually do to help a friend or family member who has a problem with addiction?

. : : : : : **Part Four** The Mechanics of Writing

In Part Five, you are going to write a persuasive paragraph about addiction. In your paragraph, you may need to use the conditional or subordinating conjunctions, and you will always want to avoid fragments. Part Four will help you to do this.

Subordinating Conjunctions: Review/Extension

In Chapters Three, Four, and Five you studied subordinating conjunctions of contrast, cause and effect, and time. This list includes both new conjunctions and those previously learned.

Cause	Time	Condition
because	when	if
since	while (= when)	unless (= if not)
as (= because)	as (= while)	
	before	
Contradiction	after	
although	until	
even though	whenever (= every time when)	
while (= although)	as soon as (= immediately after)	

As you've seen, there are two ways to use these conjunctions.

Examples: <u>Whenever</u> the child's teacher came near him, he began hurling toys at her. (comma)

The child began hurling toys at his teacher <u>whenever</u> she came near him. (no comma)

A. Understanding Subordinating Conjunctions.
Often, one word can completely change the meaning of a sentence. What is the difference in meaning between the two sentences in each pair that follows? Work with a partner to figure this out.

1*a.* I liked the fruit punch because it didn't have alcohol in it.
  b. I liked the fruit punch although it didn't have alcohol in it.

2*a.* He felt sick whenever he had a drink.
  b. He felt sick until he had a drink.

3*a.* She drank heavily until she found out she was pregnant.
  b. She drank heavily when she found out she was pregnant.

B. Sentence Combining: Subordinating Conjunctions.
Choose a logical subordinating conjunction for each item. Then combine the pairs of sentences in two ways each.

1. We'll ask her to help us with this.

   She's both knowledgeable and dependable.

   a. _____

   _____

   b. _____

   _____

2. He knew a good deal* about the danger of addiction.

   He began to use cocaine.

   (*Note: a *good deal* = a lot.)

   a. _____

   _____

   b. _____

   _____

3. Her grades in college suddenly went down.

She began taking drugs.

a. _____

_____

b. _____

_____

4. He adopted the baby.

He was informed that the birth mother was alcoholic.

a. _____

_____

b. _____

_____

5. They knew the baby had fetal alcohol syndrome.

They adopted him, anyway.

a. _____

_____

b. _____

_____

6. The baby's mother had smoked crack cocaine.

He was born.

a. _____

_____

b. _____

_____

Avoiding and Repairing Fragments

A common mistake in written (but not spoken) English is a fragment. A fragment looks like a complete sentence because it begins with a capital letter and ends with a period, but it is not complete. It is missing something.

Example: WRONG: He's addicted to drugs. For example, cocaine and heroin.

(The second "sentence" here is not really a sentence. It's a fragment because there is no subject or verb.)

CORRECTED: He's addicted to drugs. For example, he takes cocaine and heroin.

Perhaps the most common problem with fragments occurs because of the misuse of a subordinating conjunction. Remember that there must be two clauses in a sentence with a subordinating conjunction.

Example: WRONG: He can't hold a job. Because he has a problem with drugs.

(The second "sentence" is a fragment because it's missing a main clause.)

CORRECTED: He can't hold a job because he has a problem with drugs.

OR: Because he has a problem with drugs, he can't hold a job.

C. Identifying and Repairing Fragments.   Decide which "sentences" that follow are actually fragments. Then correct them. Do not change sentences that are already correct.

1. Arthur was three days old. When his aunt found him.

2. Because Arthur's crack-addicted mother had abandoned him, his aunt adopted him.

3. He wouldn't let anyone closer than eight feet. Before he began hurling toys at them.

4. Street children in many countries use psychoactive substances. Such as glue or paint thinner.

5. Children sometimes "graduate" from glue to other psychoactive substances. For example, they may later add marijuana, alcohol, cigarettes, or cocaine.

6. Indigenous people are those who were already living on their lands. When settlers came from other countries.

7. In religious ceremonies, Native Americans traditionally used hallucinogens. For example, peyote and certain types of mushrooms that helped them to have visions.

8. Because indigenous people used to have very strict laws and taboos about psychoactive substances. There wasn't such a problem in the past.

9. There wasn't much of a problem. Until indigenous people were exposed to "outside" attitudes and beliefs.

10. Many indigenous cultures are destroyed as global development occurs.

The Present Unreal Conditional

To express a situation that does not actually exist in the present time, you can use the present unreal conditional.

Examples: If I <u>knew</u> what to do, I <u>would help</u> him.

(This means: I <u>don't know</u> what to do, so I <u>don't help</u> him.)

She <u>wouldn't have</u> these problems if she <u>didn't have</u> FAS.

(This means: She <u>has</u> these problems because she <u>has</u> FAS.)

In these examples, you see that the conditional is *opposite* the real situation. In other words, if the verb in the real situation is negative, it will become affirmative in the conditional. An affirmative verb in the real situation will become negative in the conditional.

Note: *If* is one of the subordinating conjunctions, so use the same punctuation that you use with all subordinating conjunctions.

In the conditional, the *cause* is in the dependent clause with *if.* The effect or result is in the main clause; it includes *would, could,* or *might* + the simple form of the verb.

In the clause with *if,* the verb is in the past tense, but the meaning is present. If this verb is *be,* use only *were*—not *was.*

Example: If I <u>were</u> you, I'd try it.

D. Practice. In each sentence that follows, circle the *cause.* Underline the *effect* or *result.* Then change each of these real situations to the conditional. Be sure to keep the cause in the clause with *if.*

1. Magazine ads link alcohol with the idea of freedom and excitement, so many teenagers are attracted to drinking.

   _____

   _____

2. Thousands of babies are born with serious physical and mental problems because their mothers are addicted to crack cocaine.

   _____

   _____

3. People don't give up smoking, so the death rate doesn't decline. (Note: The sentence in the real situation sounds a little strange, but your conditional sentence will sound natural.)

   _____

   _____

4. Children sniff glue because it's so cheap.

_____

_____

5. There aren't taboos and laws to regulate the use of alcohol because there isn't a tradition of alcohol use in the tribe.

_____

_____

6. Street children don't trust adults, so they don't go to centers for treatment and help.

_____

_____

7. Hill tribes in Southeast Asia are now injecting opium instead of smoking it, so there is an increase in the incidence of AIDS.

_____

_____

8. It's especially important to establish treatment centers because the number of addicts is growing.

_____

_____

. . : : : : **Part Five** Writing in the Academic World

Before Writing

**A. Discussion: Gathering Ideas.**   You're going to write a paragraph about a possible solution to drug, alcohol, or tobacco abuse. To begin gathering ideas, think about the answers to these questions. (You should probably do this for homework.) Then in small groups, share your opinions. As you listen to other students, take notes on ideas different from yours.

1. What do you think about laws or government programs to prevent children and teens from smoking? Should it be illegal to sell cigarettes to anyone under a certain age? Should smoking be illegal for *everyone*? Should the government stay out of this decision? Give reasons for your answers.

2. Do you believe that alcohol should be advertised in magazines or on TV? Why or why not?

3. What should be done about women who drink or take drugs when they're pregnant? Should their children be taken away from them by the courts? (If so, temporarily? Permanently?) Should the women be sent to prison for child abuse? Should they be sent to a treatment center? Should the government stay out of this situation? Give reasons for your answer(s).

 writing **Strategy**

Writing a Topic Sentence

In a paragraph of persuasion, your topic sentence should

- be arguable—in other words, be an idea that you can support with reasons
- be an opinion, but not simply a matter of personal taste (that is, an ability to enjoy or judge something)
- not be a fact
- deal with a single point
- be limited (specific) enough for one paragraph

B. Practice.   Which of these are good topic sentences for a paragraph of persuasion? Write *good* on the line. Which are not good? On the lines write the reason they are not good. (Use the rules in the preceding box to guide you.)

_____ 1. I don't like to smoke because it makes my clothes smell terrible.

_____ 2. Consumption of heroin in the United States has doubled in the past ten years.

_____ 3. Because of the danger to everyone of passive smoke, smoking should be banned in public buildings in my country.

_____ 4. The government should stay out of people's private lives and let us make our own personal decisions.

_____ 5. The government should not have the power to interfere with a person's decision to smoke or not.

_____   **6.** Banning advertisements for alcohol from TV is a good step toward taking the glamour out of a substance that is dangerous for young people.

_____   **7.** Children have been experimenting with drugs and alcohol at younger and younger ages.

_____   **8.** Red wine is better than white wine.

_____   **9.** The sale of drugs should be legalized so that 1) the government can control the quality of these potentially dangerous substances and 2) the national economy can benefit from the taxation of drugs.

_____   **10.** In the United States, sales of beer and wine have been increasing while sales of hard liquor have been decreasing.

C. Choosing a Topic.   Choose *one* of these questions to answer in one paragraph.

- What should be done about women who drink alcohol or take drugs when they are pregnant?
- What can be done to persuade children not to begin smoking?
- What can be done to persuade children not to begin taking illicit drugs?
- Should the government be involved in the campaign to stop people from smoking?
- What is one possible solution to the problem of alcoholism?

D. Writing Your Topic Sentence.   After you've chosen one question to answer, you might decide to limit your topic to just one country—your own country, the United States, or Canada. Write your topic sentence on the following lines.

_____

_____

Before continuing, make sure that you have a good topic sentence.

- Is it arguable?
- Is it an opinion—not a fact?
- Does it deal with a single point?
- Is it limited enough for one paragraph?

E. Gathering Evidence.   On the following lines, write notes (not sentences) on evidence (support) for your topic sentence. Your evidence can be in any form that you have studied so far: example, analysis, comparison/contrast, reasons, or narration. Or it can be a combination of these methods.

_____   _____

_____   _____

_____   _____

_____   _____

_____   _____

Writing

writing **Strategy**

Writing a Persuasive Paragraph

In a persuasive paragraph, it is important to begin with a topic sentence that is arguable and limited. The rest of the paragraph gives evidence to support the opinion in the topic sentence. Your evidence can be in a variety of forms (see preceding Exercise E), but you need enough to support your opinion. The evidence must be clearly presented.

The following paragraph is one possible way to answer this question:

What can be done about the problem of drug addiction?

Example: For reasons that may appear purely economic but are essentially humane, the sale and use of illicit drugs should be legalized in the United States. First, the government cannot collect taxes on income that is made illegally, but if drugs were legalized, they could be taxed. This would be an enormous economic benefit to the country. To give one example, the largest cash crop grown in the state of California is marijuana, but the growers must now hide their profits because they are breaking the law. The taxes paid on legally grown marijuana, together with the money now spent on enforcing antidrug laws, could be spent both on education to prevent children from trying drugs and on treatment for the thousands of addicts who want to be free of their addiction. Second, legalization would cause the price of these drugs to drop. As a result, many drug pushers would choose to go out of business because it wouldn't be profitable enough. Not only would some drugs be less available than they are today, but the crime rate in general would drop as crimes associated with drug trafficking become unnecessary.

Notice in the example:

1. The topic sentence presents an arguable idea; it is not a statement of fact.

2. The topic sentence limits the topic to just one country.

3. The paragraph is limited to one kind of reason—economic. Other possible reasons have been excluded (left out).

4. The present unreal conditional is used to present a situation which does not exist.

Writing Assignment: First Draft.   Go back to your notes for evidence (page 215). Cross out anything that doesn't stay on target. Then write your paragraph, writing your notes in the form of complete sentences.

After Writing

A. Self-Check.   Read over your paragraph. Answer the questions on the checklist. Write yes or no.

B. Classmate's Check.   Exchange papers with a classmate. Check each other's paragraphs. Write yes or no on your classmate's checklist.

editing Checklist

Points To Check For	My Check	My Classmate's Check
1. Is the paragraph form correct (indentation, margins)?	_____	_____
2. Is the topic sentence arguable?	_____	_____
3. Is the topic sentence opinion, not fact?	_____	_____
4. Is the topic limited enough for one paragraph?	_____	_____
5. Is there clearly presented evidence?	_____	_____
6. If there is use of the present unreal conditional, is the grammar correct?	_____	_____
7. Have fragments been avoided?	_____	_____
8. Other: _____	_____	_____

Second Draft.   Use the answers on your checklist to guide you in your revision. Rewrite your paragraph and give it to your teacher.

chapter Eight

Secrets of Good Health

In this chapter, you will consider various ways to retain and regain good health. You'll write a paragraph of definition about one aspect of health.

. : : : : : **Part One** Ten Principles of Health and Illness

Before Reading

A. Discussion. In small groups, look over the quotations in the box and discuss them. If there are some words that you don't know, ask someone in your group or check with a dictionary.

1. Is there one quotation that you especially like? Why?

2. Is there a famous proverb about health from your culture? If so, think of how to say it in English and share it with your group.

Early to bed and early to rise, makes a man healthy, wealthy, and wise.
—Benjamin Franklin, *Poor Richard's Almanak*

There is a limit to the best of health; disease is always a near neighbor.
—Aeschylus, *Agamemnon*

Cured yesterday of my disease, I died last night of the physician.
—Matthew Prior, *The Remedy Worse than the Disease*

Natural forces within us are the true healers of disease.
—Hippocrates, *Aphorisms*

Look into the depths of your own soul and learn first to know yourself, then you will understand why this illness was bound to come upon you and perhaps you will . . . avoid falling ill.
—Sigmund Freud, *One of the Difficulties of Psychoanalysis*

Keep breathing. [key to long life]
—Sophie Tucker (American singer)

Reading

As you read the following passage by a medical doctor, think about the answer to this question.

• What do you *expect* a doctor to say about health and illness?

Ten Principles of Health and Illness

1. Perfect Health Is Not Attainable

Health is only temporary, destined to break down so that it can be reestablished as the foundation it rests on changes. Change is the essence of life. Periods of breakdown of equilibrium are periods of relative illness between peaks of relative health. Perfect health is an impossibility.

"Periods of relative illness" does not necessarily mean being sick in bed, or going to a hospital, or having to call a doctor. Relative illness can be as minor as a headache, a lack of energy, a night of restless sleep, a tiny injury. In fact, the valleys between new equilibrations may be so small that some persons might not call them illness and others might not even notice them.

2. It Is All Right to Be Sick

I think it is fine to regard relative sickness as undesired and to work with all effort and intelligence toward reducing its severity and duration. We must not reject it as something that should not happen, however. Sickness is the way to the next relative period of health, and one state cannot exist without the other, any more than day can exist without night.

3. The Body Has Innate Healing Abilities

Healing comes from inside, not outside. It is simply the body's natural attempt to restore equilibrium when equilibrium is lost. You are born with the power to heal because healing is an innate capacity of every person, as it is of every animal and plant.

4. Agents of Disease Are Not Causes of Disease

Not everyone who meets up with the flu virus gets flu, probably for many possible reasons. Agents of disease do not cause us to get sick. Agents of disease are all around us, not only in the form of viruses, bacteria, and parasites but as a multitude of potential irritants, such as chemicals, allergens, insects, toxic plants, and so forth. A person in a phase of relative health can often interact with these agents and not get sick.

Material objects are never causes of disease, merely agents waiting to cause specific symptoms. Rather than warring on disease agents, we ought to worry more about strengthening resistance to them and learning to live in balance with them more of the time.

5. All Illness Is Psychosomatic

Psychosomatic means "mind-body," nothing more. It does not mean "unreal" or "not serious" or "not physical." To say that all illness is psychosomatic is to say only that all illness has both physical and mental components. How could it be otherwise? All illness is psychosomatic because we are mind-bodies, not just bodies.

6. Subtle Manifestations of Illness Precede Gross Ones

All creations start small and grow, including conditions of disease. Failure to notice and recognize disease at early stages is one of the main reasons for its severity and stubbornness. The earlier you notice a medical problem, the less work will be needed to correct it.

Unless you learn to notice and be bothered by the early, subtle stages of illness, you will lose your chances of managing your body through its changing cycles and will find yourself more and more dependent on modern hospital medicine.

7. Every Body Is Different

Biochemical individuality is one reason for variations in responses to drugs—a fact not much emphasized in medical teaching. There is probably a best treatment for any individual with a particular problem, but what is best for me might not be best for you even if our problems appear similar. As a generalization, the universal treatment or the perfect system of medicine is as much a fantasy as the perfect diet.

8. Every Body Has a Weak Point

Bodies have one or more weak points. It is useful to know those points because they tend to register stress as early warnings of breakdowns in health. Learn your weak points. They will give you signals. Practice at recognizing those signals will help you notice illness in its subtle stages and improve your chances of correcting it by simple measures.

9. Blood Is a Principal Carrier of Healing Energy

A healthy circulatory system, with adequate and normal blood, is the keystone of the body's healing system. One of the most effective ways to promote healing, if it can be done, is to increase the amount of blood reaching an ailing part of the body.

10. Proper Breathing Is a Key to Good Health

Breath is the most vital and most mysterious function. Breathing is a bridge between the mind and body. Proper breathing nourishes the central nervous system, establishes a harmonious pattern for other bodily rhythms, and also regulates moods and emotions. By "proper breathing" I mean full, deep expansion of the lungs. Learning how to breath and working consciously with breath is a simple, safe, effective, and inexpensive way to promote good health of mind and body.

After Reading

A. Vocabulary Check.   Look back at "Ten Principles of Health and Illness" to find words for these definitions. Numbers in parentheses refer to numbers of principles.

1. a condition of balance (1): _____

2. high points (1): _____

3. low points (1): _____

4. seriousness, strength (2): _____

5. (adjective) having an ability that one was born with (3): _____

6. things that work to produce a result (4): _____

7. things that bother or irritate (4): _____

8. parts (5): _____

9. small and difficult to notice (6): _____

10. organs in the chest with which we breathe (10): _____

B. Application.   Look back at the quotations in the box on page 218. Which quotations seem to agree with (or restate) these principles?

• Perfect health is not attainable.

   Quotation: _____

   _____

• The body has innate healing abilities.

   Quotation: _____

   _____

• All illness is psychosomatic.

   Quotation: _____

   _____

• Proper breathing is a key to good health.

   Quotation: _____

   _____

C. Discussion.   In small groups, discuss these questions.

1. Were you surprised by any of Dr. Weil's ten principles? If so, which ones?

2. What do *you* think are the most important principles of good health?

D. Response Writing.   For ten minutes, write on *one* of these topics. Don't stop writing to use a dictionary or to worry about grammar.

- your response to one of the quotations on page 218

- your response to one of Dr. Weil's ten principles

- your ideas about the most important things that people can do to stay healthy

. : : : : : **Part Two** Secrets of a Long Life:
                     "Attention, Willard Scott"

Before Reading

A. Vocabulary Preparation.   The following article has some words that will be new to you. What can you guess about each underlined word that follows? Write your guess on each line. Then compare your answers with another student's.

1. She was driving down the street when suddenly her car hit a <u>pothole</u>. The car wasn't damaged, but she was a little shaken. The city government needs to hire more people to fix these holes, especially in the rainy season.

   My Guess: _____

2. The expression on his face was an absolute <u>deadpan</u>, so we had no idea if he was serious or joking.

   My Guess: _____

3. I went to bed really late last night. The book I was reading was so <u>intriguing</u> that I couldn't put it down.

   My Guess: _____

4. <u>Roughly</u> 80 percent of these people are white; about 50 percent live alone or with family members.

   My Guess: _____

5. My grandfather has a very <u>upbeat outlook</u> on life. It's refreshing to be around him. A lot of people in my family seem to complain all the time and be awfully negative, but he's always had this positive attitude.

My Guess: _____

6. Her doctor told her to cut down on drinking and to stop smoking completely, but she's <u>defying</u> her doctor's orders. She still has a few glasses of wine every day and smokes like a chimney.

My Guess: _____

B. Discussion.   In small groups, answer these questions.

1. In your country, is *life expectancy* (that is, the age that people can expect to reach) going up or down? What are reasons for this?

2. Do you know anyone who is very, very old and still healthy? If so, does he or she do anything unusual to remain healthy at this age?

C. Thinking Ahead.   What things should we do (or not do) if we want to live a very long, healthy life? Brainstorm this question in small groups and write your answers here, in note form.

Do	**Not Do**
_____	_____
_____	_____
_____	_____
_____	_____
_____	_____
_____	_____

Reading

A. Making Predictions.   The subtitle of the following article is "More and more people are living to see 100." Also, you see a picture of a healthy 100-year-old woman in a dance class. What question would you like the article to answer? Write it here.

_____

_____

B. Skimming for Important Information.   Now quickly skim the article "Attention, Willard Scott." *This should take you only about one minute.* Look for the answer to your question in Exercise A (Making Predictions). If you find the answer, highlight it with a felt-tip pen. Then wait for everyone to finish and compare your answer with other students'.

C. Reading for Main Ideas.   As you read the article, think about the answers to these questions.

• What do most centenarians seem to have in common? (How are they similar?)

• What are some *other* explanations for long life?

Attention, Willard Scott

More and More People Are Living to See 100

At 100 years and 5 months old, Claire Willi takes a dance class every day and is as elegant as she is energetic. Accidentally nudged into a deep pothole recently, she climbed out on
5 her own and proceeded to her hairdresser, who obligingly cleaned her white suit. At 101, Harry Schneider is so sharp he can recall the weekly salaries of his youth. "You want me to start with when I came to America? My story
10 takes a long time," says the Russian emigre. Ask Lizzie Norman how it feels to be 100 and a slow smile spreads over her wrinkled black face. Does she regret not getting a card from the president on her birthday? Norman dead-
15 pans: "Put a 50 in it and I'll take it."

Willi dancing at 100.

Of all the measures of America's aging population, none is more intriguing than the rising number of centenarians. The U.S. Census Bureau counted 35,808 people 100 years and older in 1990—double the number 10 years ago—and there could be 1 million by 2080, given the expanding population and longer life expect-
20 ancy. But that's just the Census's best guess: arriving at an exact count is surprisingly difficult. The Social Security Administration lists roughly 32,000 centenarians on its rolls, including some with impossibly high ages. "We know . . . these people aren't 150 years old, but as long as they could prove they were at least 65 when social security started 40 years ago, we don't make them prove exactly how old

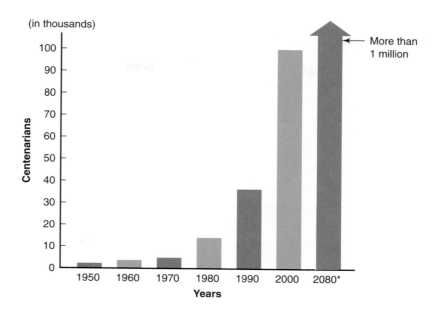

25 they are," says press officer Phil Gambino. Even the White House can be duped in its effort to send birthday greetings to very old Americans. White House volunteers rely on friends and families to request greetings, and don't try to verify them. Recently someone obtained a card for a "best friend"—a dog, allegedly 100 in dog years.

30   Whatever their exact numbers, human centenarians are the focus of increasing research. Women over 100 outnumber men about 2 to 1, according to a 1987 National Institute of Aging report. Roughly 80 percent are white, though proportionally more blacks live to be older than 105. About half reside alone or with family members. The odds against living to be 100, the NIA noted, have dropped from 400 35 to 1 for people born in 1879 to a mere 87 to 1 for those born in 1980.

     What's the secret of living so long? David Wekstein at the University of Kentucky's Sanders-Brown Center on Aging studied 546 centenarians and found that most had a close relationship with a spouse, a child, or a nursing-home staffer. Most had upbeat outlooks on life—and many had avoided caffeine, alcohol, and 40 tobacco. "It's as if they read the books by the American Heart Association and the American Cancer Society and lived their lives accordingly," Wekstein says. Others, however, defy the conventional wisdom. "I never took any medicine. I took Scotch, 95 years, every day of the week—and I was never drunk," declares Harry Schneider. In his 1990 book *One Hundred Over 100,* author Jim Heynen profiled some cente-45 narians who had recovered repeatedly from cancer; some were chronic worriers, some weighed 245 pounds and many had spent their lives helping others. Ruth Inez Austin, for example, became a career social worker after being arrested in a 1920s garment-workers strike for hitting a policeman with her muff.

Another unscientific measure of the century club's growth comes from NBC's
50 *Today* show, which has been airing birthday wishes to Americans 100 and older since the mid-1980s. Willard Scott now gets about 50 requests for greetings every day—double the number five years ago.

Centenarians offer explanations of their longevity as varied as their life stories. Claire Willi credits her exercise regime: "Stand straight—it's very important."
55 Henry Neligan, a British sailor who survived two shipwrecks, told Heynen: "Keep your feet warm, your head cool, your bowels open, and trust in the Lord." Robert Coulter, 106, who came from Ireland on the *Lusitania* and spent 30 years on Ford assembly lines, credits his parents. "If you plant a strong plant," he says, "it grows."

After Reading

A. Main Ideas.   In small groups, answer these questions.

1. What seem to be three secrets of living a long, healthy life?

2. How do these people explain their longevity?

Harry Schneider	
Claire Willi	
Henry Neligan	
Robert Coulter	

B. Vocabulary Check.   Find a word or expression in the article for each definition that follows. The numbers in parentheses refer to lines.

1. pushed (1–5): _____

2. continued on (5–10): _____

3. people who are 100 or older (15–20): _____

4. a government agency that collects information about the population (15–20): _____

5. live (30–35): _____

6. long life (50–55): _____

7. program (50–55): _____

8. terrible accidents on the ocean (50–55): _____

reading Strategy

Understanding Possessive Adjectives

Frequently, a possessive adjective refers back to a "nearby" noun.

Example: Claire Willi credits <u>her</u> exercise regime.

("her" = Claire Willi's)

To understand many possessive adjectives, however, it is necessary to look back to a noun quite far from the possessive adjective—perhaps in a previous sentence.

Example: At 100 years and 5 months old, Claire Willi takes a dance class every day and is as elegant as she is energetic. Accidentally nudged into a deep pothole recently, she climbed out on her own and proceeded to <u>her</u> hairdresser.

(The word <u>her</u> refers back first to the previous "her," then to "she," and then to the subject in the previous sentence, Claire Willi.)

Occasionally, a possessive adjective refers to a noun that comes *after* it.

Example: In <u>his</u> 1990 book *One Hundred Over 100*, author Jim Heynen profiled some centenarians who had recovered repeatedly from cancer.

(<u>his</u> = Jim Heynen's)

C. Reference. What does each possessive adjective refer to? (You will need to look back at the article.) Write the noun on the line.

1. his (line 8)   = _____

2. her (line 14)   = _____

3. their (line 41) = _____

4. their (line 46) = _____

5. her (line 48)   = _____

6. his (line 58)   = _____

D. Making Inferences. In small groups, make inferences to answer these questions. (You will need to look back at the context.)

1. Was Claire Willi driving or walking when she was nudged into the pothole (first paragraph)? How do you know?

2. At the end of the first paragraph, Lizzie Norman deadpans, "Put a 50 in it and I'll take it." What does "it" refer to? What do you think Norman means by "a 50"?

3. The fourth paragraph tells us: ". . . Jim Heynen profiled some centenarians who had recovered repeatedly from cancer; some were chronic worriers, some weighed 245 pounds and many had spent their lives helping others." What can you infer from this information?

. : ∶ ⋮ ⋮ Part Three Reading in the Academic World

Before Reading

A. Vocabulary Preparation. The following passage, written by Dr. Andrew Weil, has some words that will be new to you. You can understand something about many of them from the context. What can you guess about each underlined word that follows? Write your guess for each word; compare your answers with another student's. Then check with a dictionary for any of these words that you feel very unsure about.

1. I couldn't <u>grasp</u> what he meant. His ideas were so new to me, so complex and strange, that I had difficulty understanding his meaning.

My Guess: _____

2. A knowledge of basic math is <u>fundamental</u> to a study of calculus or other higher mathematics.

My Guess: _____

3. The word *psychotherapy* <u>derives</u> from two Greek roots that mean "mind" and "treatment."

My Guess: _____

4. In Western medicine, medical doctors usually treat only physical <u>ailments</u> while psychiatrists and psychologists deal with mental illness.

My Guess: _____

5. I hate going to a medical clinic. Usually, when I get the flu, I stay home. I sleep a lot, drink a lot of liquid, and take aspirin. If this doesn't work, my final <u>recourse</u> is to go to the doctor.

My Guess: _____

6. The police know who the kidnappers are, but they can't find their <u>whereabouts</u>.

My Guess: _____

7. Our vision was <u>obscured</u> by the trees, so we couldn't see the lake from our window.

My Guess: _____

8. We <u>integrated</u> many people's ideas into our final plan.

My Guess: _____

B. Thinking Ahead.   With a partner, look at and discuss the *caduceus,* the symbol of the medical profession. You see a winged staff with two intertwined snakes. This symbol was associated with the Greek god Hermes, the messenger of the gods.

1. Is this a medical symbol in your culture, also?

2. Can you think of a possible explanation for the symbolism of the two intertwined snakes? What might they mean?

C. Making Predictions.   In small groups, brainstorm the answer to this question: How many definitions of the word *health* can you think of?

Reading

As you read this passage from *Health and Healing,* think about the answer to these questions.

1. Where does the word *health* come from?

2. According to Dr. Weil, why is the caduceus an appropriate symbol of the medical profession?

Health as Wholeness; Wholeness as Perfection

We know health well in its absence.

When we are sick or injured we have no trouble knowing how things should be. A pain should not be there. An arm should move freely.
5 A rash should go away. "Freedom from disease" is a common dictionary definition of health. Since *disease* comes from an Old French word meaning "lack of ease," we are left with a doubly negative sense: health is the absence of an
10 absence of ease.

We talk about our health much of the time. (Some people talk about it most of the time.) We spend a great deal of money trying to restore it or improve it. We join health clubs, visit health
15 resorts, buy health foods. Yet in my years of formal medical education I never heard a good answer to the question, "What is health?" Many modern doctors cannot grasp the true meaning of health and can only define it negatively as
20 freedom from disease. What the word really signifies is much more interesting.

I will examine some deep and perhaps unfamiliar ideas. These ideas are fundamental to the practical discussions of treatment coming
25 later. Whenever possible, I will give concrete examples in order to show their relevance.

The root meaning of *health* is "wholeness." The word comes from the same Anglo-Saxon root that gives us *whole, hale,* and *holy.*
30 *Cure* and *care* come from one and the same Latin root: to cure is to take care of. *Treat* has a similar root meaning in Old French: to deal with or manage toward some particular end. *Medicine* comes from Latin *medicina,* and that
35 word derives from an ancient Indo-European root that has also given us *remedy, meditate,* and *measure.* The root seems to suggest "thoughtful action to establish order. Thus *cure, treatment,* and *medicine* all suggest action to restore some
40 aspect of wholeness implied by the word *health.*

Native American medicine men are religious leaders as much as doctors, treating spiritual and physical ailments at one and the same time. They often speak of the Medicine Wheel
45 as the basis of tribal health, drawing on the circle as a universal symbol of wholeness and perfection.

In the Western tradition, one of the best symbols of this same idea is the caduceus, or
50 wand of Hermes, the familiar winged staff with its intertwined snakes.

Medical historians sometimes say that the caduceus should not be the doctor's emblem, that it became so by confusion with another
55 symbol, the staff of Asklepios, a plain staff with a single snake around it. Asklepios was the patron god of physicians in Ancient Greece. Both doctors and patients offered sacrifices to him, and the final recourse of the very sick was to go
60 to his temple, called the Asklepion. Snakes were sacred to Asklepios and so were allowed to roam his temples freely. The ritual of the Asklepion was simple: The sick would lie down in the great hall, listen to the hymns of the priests, and wait
65 for night. Then they would stay until the god appeared to them in dreams and gave advice.

But I consider the caduceus a far more appropriate symbol. The talents of Hermes—his speed, knowledge, effectiveness, and ability to
70 protect from evil—all depend on his practical use of one chief secret: that power flows freely when the opposites of existence are woven into the perfect pattern. That pattern appears in the caduceus. The two snakes are the light and the
75 dark, good and evil, yang and yin.

In most societies throughout most of history, magic, religion, and medicine have been intertwined, practiced together, and seen as having a common origin. The shaman of tribal
80 peoples in northern Asia and the Americas is the doctor of bodies, souls, and situations. He (or she) has learned to be a personal mediator between the everyday world and the "other world," leaving his body to commune with spirits and
85 learn the specific causes of illness, the whereabouts of missing objects, the reasons for failures of crops.

In our society, the commonality of religion, magic, and medicine is obscured. Our medical
90 doctors have narrowed their view to pay attention only to the physical body and the material aspects of illness. As a result, they cannot practice the healing magic of Hermes because they do not see or integrate the nonphysical forces
95 that animate and direct the physical body. For the same reason, many doctors cannot come up with a better definition of health than "absence of disease." They do not grasp the concept of wholeness as perfection that is the root meaning
100 of the word.

After Reading

A. Comprehension Check. With a partner, discuss the answers to these questions.

1. In Native American culture, what is a symbol (and the basis) of health? Why?

2. According to Dr. Weil, what do the two snakes on the caduceus symbolize?

3. Why might the snakes on the caduceus be an appropriate symbol of magic, religion, and medicine in most societies?

B. Identifying Definitions.   In this passage, Andrew Weil attempts to define *health*. Look back at the passage to find these meanings. When you find them, mark them with a felt-tip pen.

1. What is a common dictionary definition of *health*?

2. How can this definition be "translated"? In other words, what is the real meaning of this definition?

3. What is the root meaning of *health*?

4. What is the word *health* derived from?

C. Vocabulary Expansion.   Use a dictionary to help you find other parts of speech of these words from the passage.

Nouns	Adjectives	Verbs
1. _____	_____	derive
2. _____	_____	restore
3. ailment	_____	_____
4. _____	_____	signify
5. medicine medication	_____	_____

D. Vocabulary Check.   Look back at the passage to find words for these definitions.

1. an object (such as the caduceus) that symbolizes something else = _____

2. two opposite principles (in Chinese philosophy)
   of light and dark, good and evil, and so on = _____

E. Word Journal.   Go back to the passage. Which words are important for you to remember? Put them in your Word Journal.

F. Discussion.   In small groups, answer these questions.

1. What is the word for *health* in your language? Does it have a root meaning?

2. Dr. Weil mentions three symbols of health in the meaning of "wholeness": the Native American Medicine Wheel, the caduceus, and the yin/yang pattern. Do you have these or any other symbols of wholeness in your culture? If so, explain them.

Native American medicine wheel

Yin/Yang pattern

3. What do you think about the doctor in this cartoon? Why? (Note: "That thing that's going around" is an informal way of referring to a contagious illness, such as the flu, which many people are catching.)

Beetle Bailey

G. Making Inferences.   Dr. Weil implies that many modern medical doctors do not fully understand what *health* is and, therefore, ignore the emotional or spiritual needs of their patients. Find phrases and sentences from which you can infer this. Then compare your answers with other students'.

:::: **Part Four** The Mechanics of Writing

In Part Five, you are going to write a paragraph of definition. You have already studied the use of adjective clauses (relative clauses) in definitions (Chapter One and Chapter Six). In your paragraph, however, you may also need to use italics and quotation marks and to combine ideas by using conjunctions. Part Four will help you with this.

Summary of the Use of Italics and Quotation Marks

Four ways in which writers use italics in academic writing are

- for the title of a book, movie, newspaper, or magazine
- for emphasis
- for a foreign word used in an English sentence
- when they mean "the word . . ." or "the term . . ."

Examples: In *Health and Healing,* Dr. Weil offers a refreshingly balanced point of view. (title of a book)

He lived not only long but *well.* (emphasis)

In Africa, the use of *khat* is part of everyday life for some people. (foreign word in an English sentence)

Psychosomatic means "mind-body." (= the *word* psychosomatic)

Four ways in which writers use quotation (quote) marks in academic writing are

- for a direct quotation of someone's exact words
- for the meaning of a word
- for the title of a short story, short poem, or newspaper or magazine article
- when they are using a term differently from its usual meaning

Examples: "Keep your feet warm," he recommends. (direct quotation)

The root meaning of the word is "wholeness." (meaning of a word)

In "Attention, Willard Scott," we discovered that more and more people are living to 100. (title of a magazine article)

Many families rely on intervention to "wake up" an addicted person from the state of denial. (a term used differently from usual)

A. Identifying the Meaning of Italics and Quotation Marks.   In each blank write the reason for the use of italics or quotation marks.

1. _____ The root of the word seems to suggest "thoughtful action to establish order."

2. _____ It's time for him to "face the music" and admit his problem with addiction.

3. _____ I absolutely *craved* some ice cream.

4. _____ People in drug recovery describe themselves as "recovering" instead of "recovered."

5. _____ In *The Broken Cord,* Michael Dorris describes the difficulty of raising a child born with FAS.

6. _____ *Treat* is derived from an Old French word.

7. _____ It does not mean "unreal" or "not serious."

8. _____ They drank a few glasses of *ouzo.*

Using Quotation Marks and Italics

Make sure to put quote marks around all words from another source but not around your own words. It is possible to put the attribution (i.e., who said this) in the middle of the quote, but if you do this, you need two sets (pairs) of quote marks. If your attribution is at the end of a quoted sentence, a comma comes before the end quote marks. Notice the punctuation in these examples.

Examples: According to Andrew Weil, "It's all right to be sick."

"If you plant a strong plant," he says, "it grows."

"All illness is psychosomatic," Andrew Weil tells us.

If you use a typewriter or handwriting, underline anything that would be in italics on a computer.

Examples: Psychosomatic means "mind-body."

Psychosomatic means "mind-body."

B. Using Quotation Marks and Italics.   Add quotation marks where necessary in this paragraph. Also, underline anything that should be in italics. When you finish, compare your punctuation with that of another student.

> Good health means much more than not sick. More and more health experts these days are pointing out that health includes our state of mind and is—to a large extent—the responsibility of each individual because as Dr. Andrew Weil points out, Every body is different. We need to learn to recognize the subtle changes in our physical health and also in our kefi—a Greek word that means mood or spirit. We are mind-bodies, Dr. Weil tells us in his book Health and Healing. For this reason, it isn't enough to ignore the nonphysical elements of health.

Review of Conjunctions

There are often many ways to express the same idea. Knowing how to connect sentences in several ways is one technique to using variety in your writing. In previous chapters you studied the three types of conjunctions: coordinating, subordinating, and adverbial.

As a review, notice how you can express a relationship of contradiction or cause and effect in various ways.

	Contradiction	Cause and Effect
Coordinating Conjunctions	but yet (= but)	so (= that's why) for (= because)
Subordinating Conjunctions	although even though while (= although)	because since (= because) as (= because)
Adverbial Conjunctions	however nevertheless even so	therefore as a result consequently ⎱ (= so) for this reason ⎰ thus

Compare the punctuation in these sentences.

Examples: Many people believe that psychosomatic illnesses are unreal, but this is inaccurate.

Although many people believe that psychosomatic illnesses are unreal, this is inaccurate.

Many people believe that psychosomatic illnesses are unreal; however, this is inaccurate.

C. Sentence Combining: Conjunctions.   Combine these pairs of sentences in three ways each—
with a coordinating conjunction (C), a subordinating conjunction (S), and an adverbial conjunction (A).

1. Illness may be as minor as a headache or a lack of energy.

Some people might not even notice that they are ill.

C: _____

_____

S: _____

_____

A: _____

_____

2. We should work toward reducing the severity and duration of sickness.

We must not reject sickness as something that shouldn't happen.

C: _____

_____

S: _____

_____

A: _____

_____

3. Healing is an innate ability of every living thing.

You have the power to heal yourself.

C: _____

_____

S: _____

_____

A: _____

_____

4. Many healthy centenarians have avoided caffeine, alcohol, and tobacco.

Others seem to have "broken all the rules."

C: _____

_____

S: _____

_____

A: _____

_____

5. Unfortunately, most medical doctors pay attention just to the physical body.

They seem able to define *good health* only as "absence of disease."

C: _____

_____

S: _____

_____

A: _____

_____

.∴∷ Part Five Writing in the Academic World

Before Writing

A. Brainstorming.   You are going to write a paragraph of definition. In small groups, brainstorm your ideas about the following terms. What do *you* think each term means? As you listen to the other students give their opinions, take notes on ideas different from yours.

1. a physician _____

2. cancer _____

3. a healer _____

4. equilibrium _____

5. longevity _____

6. yin and yang _____

writing Strategy

Writing a Definition

Frequently, especially on essay exams, you will need to define terms. You can clearly explain what something means by using a variety of methods. Here are eight types of definitions, with examples of each.

1. synonym

peaks = high points

longevity = long life

2. dictionary definition

deadpan = "with no show of feeling, especially when telling jokes" (*Longman Dictionary of American English*)

innate = "existing in one from birth" (*Random House Dictionary of the English Language*)

3. your own definition

outlook = an attitude or way of looking at something

4. classification

TERM		GLASS (GROUP)	DIFFERENTIATION
Chronobiology	is	a science	that examines the effect of time on living systems.
A centenarian	is	a person	who lives to be 100.*

5. function

A census bureau collects population figures.

A doctor heals people.

6. etymology (the origin or history of a word)

The word *centenarian* comes from the Latin *cent,* which means "hundred."

Chronobiology is derived from three Greek roots: *chron,* meaning "time," *bio* ("life"), and *-logy* ("study").

7. **negation**

Beauty is not just an attractive appearance.

A "period of relative illness" does not necessarily mean being sick in bed or having to call a doctor.

8. **example**

An example of a serious illness is cancer.

Claire Willi, Harry Schneider, and Lizzie Norman are examples of centenarians who have not only lived long but also *well*.

* Note: To review the rules for adjective clauses, check Chapter One, page 26.

B. Identifying Definitions.   Look back at the reading passage "Health as Wholeness; Wholeness as Perfection," in Part Three. How many types of definitions can you find? Mark them with a felt-tip pen and write the type of definition (synonym, negation, etc.) in the margin.

C. Gathering Information.   For each term that follows, write as many types of definitions as possible. Try to have four or five definitions for each. (You will need to consult a dictionary for etymology and dictionary definitions.)

1. physician

_____

_____

_____

_____

_____

2. cancer

_____

_____

_____

_____

_____

3. healer

_____

_____

_____

_____

_____

4. equilibrium

_____

_____

_____

_____

_____

5. longevity

_____

_____

_____

_____

_____

6. yin and yang

_____

_____

_____

_____

_____

Writing

writing Strategy

Writing a Paragraph of Definition

In writing a paragraph of definition, you will use as many types of definitions as necessary to explain a word or term clearly. The specific types of definitions that you choose depend on the word you are explaining.

Here is one possible paragraph of definition for the word *psychosomatic*.

Example: The word *psychosomatic* is derived from two Greek roots—*psych*, meaning "mind" and *soma*, meaning "body." Many people believe that a psychosomatic illness is one that exists simply in the imagination of the patient and is, therefore, unreal. As Andrew Weil points out in *Health and Healing*, however, this is not true. He tells us that "all illness has both physical and mental components." For example, a student might have a headache caused by tension in her neck and shoulder muscles, but what causes the tense muscles? Maybe the cause is worry over midterm exams, an argument with a friend, or family problems—in other words, her mind. An elderly man has a number of physical symptoms, all due to poor diet, but what caused the poor diet? It may have been caused by depression after the death of his wife—again, his mind. In short, we see that every psychosomatic sickness has both physical and mental elements because every person has both a mind and a body.

Notice in the preceding paragraph:

- There is one definition by etymology.
- There is negation.
- Quotation marks are around the definition taken from another source.
- The source—Andrew Weil—is cited (given credit).
- There are two lengthy examples.
- A conclusion summarizes the paragraph.

Writing Assignment: First Draft.   Go back to the Gathering Information section (Exercise C on page 240). Choose *one* of the terms that you defined and write a paragraph of definition. You will need to decide if it is appropriate to use all of your definitions or just some. Include at least three types of definitions, however. One of your three should be example(s).

After Writing

A. Self-Check.   Read over your paragraph. Answer the questions on the checklist. Write *yes* or *no*.

B. Classmate's Check.   Exchange papers with a classmate. Check each other's paragraphs. Write *yes* or *no* on your classmate's checklist.

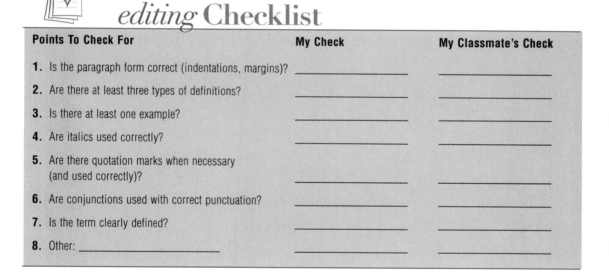

editing Checklist

Points To Check For	My Check	My Classmate's Check
1. Is the paragraph form correct (indentations, margins)?	_____	_____
2. Are there at least three types of definitions?	_____	_____
3. Is there at least one example?	_____	_____
4. Are italics used correctly?	_____	_____
5. Are there quotation marks when necessary (and used correctly)?	_____	_____
6. Are conjunctions used with correct punctuation?	_____	_____
7. Is the term clearly defined?	_____	_____
8. Other: _____	_____	_____

Second Draft.   Use the answers on your checklist to guide you in your revision. Rewrite your paragraph and give it to your teacher.

appendix 1
Spelling Rules

Rules for adding an -s for the plural form and the third person singular of verbs in the simple present tense:

1. Add *-es* to words that end in *-ch, -s, -sh, -x,* or *-z.*

catch	$\longrightarrow$	catches
kiss	$\longrightarrow$	kisses
push	$\longrightarrow$	pushes
fix	$\longrightarrow$	fixes
buzz	$\longrightarrow$	buzzes

2. If the simple form of a verb ends in a consonant + *y,* change the *y* to *i* and add *-es.*

fly	$\longrightarrow$	flies
study	$\longrightarrow$	studies

   Note: Do not change the *y* or add an *e* if the simple form ends in vowel + *y.*

enjoy	$\longrightarrow$	enjoys
stay	$\longrightarrow$	stays

3. For most other verbs, just add *-s.*

think	$\longrightarrow$	thinks
put	$\longrightarrow$	puts

Rules for adding *-ing:*

1. If the simple form of the verb ends in a silent *-e,* drop the *-e* and add *-ing.*

move	$\longrightarrow$	moving
write	$\longrightarrow$	writing

2. If the simple form ends in *-ie,* drop the *-ie,* add *y* and then *-ing.*

die	$\longrightarrow$	dying
lie	$\longrightarrow$	lying

3. If the last three letters are consonant/vowel/consonant in a one-syllable word, double the last consonant and then add *-ing.*

put	$\longrightarrow$	putting
run	$\longrightarrow$	running
drop	$\longrightarrow$	dropping

   Note: Do not double *w, x,* or *y.*

4. For a two-syllable word that ends in consonant/vowel/consonant, there are two rules:

   a. If the accent is on the second syllable, double the final consonant.

permit	$\longrightarrow$	permitting

b. If the accent is on the first syllable, do not double the final consonant.

> happen ⟶ happening

5. For all other verbs, simply add *-ing.* Do not drop, add, or change anything.

> work ⟶ working
>
> study ⟶ studying

Rules for adding *-ed* for the past tense or past participle of regular verbs:

1. If the verb already ends in *-e,* just add *-d.*

> move ⟶ moved
>
> tie ⟶ tied

2. If the verb ends in consonant + *y,* change the *y* to *-ied.*

> hurry ⟶ hurried
>
> study ⟶ studied

Note: Do not change the *y* to *-ied* if the verb ends in vowel + *y.*

> enjoy ⟶ enjoyed
>
> stay ⟶ stayed

3. If the last three letters are consonant/vowel/consonant in a one-syllable word, double the last consonant and then add *-ed.*

> rub ⟶ rubbed
>
> stop ⟶ stopped

Note: Do not double *w, x,* or *y.*

4. For a two-syllable word that ends in consonant/vowel/consonant, there are two rules:

a. If the accent is on the second syllable, double the final consonant.

> permit ⟶ permitted

b. If the accent is on the first syllable, do not double the final consonant.

> happen ⟶ happened

5. For all other regular verbs, simply add *-ed.*

> learn ⟶ learned
>
> want ⟶ wanted

appendix 2
Common Irregular Verbs

be am-is-are, was-were, been
beat, beat, beaten
become, became, become
begin, began, begun
bend, bent, bent
bet, bet, bet
bleed, bled, bled
blow, blew, blown
break, broke, broken
bring, brought, brought
build, built, built
burst, burst, burst
buy, bought, bought
catch, caught, caught
choose, chose, chosen
come, came, come
cost, cost, cost
creep, crept, crept
cut, cut, cut
dig, dug, dug
dive, dove *or* dived, dived
do, did, done
draw, drew, drawn
drink, drank, drunk
drive, drove, driven
eat, ate, eaten
fall, fell, fallen
feed, fed, fed
feel, felt, felt
fight, fought, fought
find, found, found
fit, fit, fit
flee, fled, fled
fly, flew, flown
forget, forgot, forgotten

freeze, froze, frozen
get, got, got *or* gotten
give, gave, given
go, went, gone
grind, ground, ground
grow, grew, grown
hang, hung, hung
have, had, had
hear, heard, heard
hide, hid, hidden
hit, hit, hit
hold, held, held
hurt, hurt, hurt
keep, kept, kept
know, knew, known
lay, laid, laid
lead, led, led
leave, left, left
lend, lent, lent
let, let, let
lie, lay, lain
lose, lost, lost
make, made, made
mean, meant, meant
meet, met, met
pay, paid, paid
put, put, put
read, read, read
ride, rode, ridden
ring, rang, rung
rise, rose, risen
run, ran, run
say, said, said
see, saw, seen
sell, sold, sold
send, sent, sent

set, set, set
sew, sewed, sewn
shake, shook, shaken
shine, shone, shone
shoot, shot, shot
show, showed, shown
shrink, shrank, shrunk
shut, shut, shut
sing, sang, sung
sink, sank, sunk
sit, sat, sat
sleep, slept, slept
speak, spoke, spoken
spend, spent, spent
split, split, split
spread, spread, spread
stand, stood, stood
steal, stole, stolen
stick, stuck, stuck
strike, struck, struck
swear, swore, sworn
sweep, swept, swept
swim, swam, swum
take, took, taken
teach, taught, taught
tear, tore, torn
tell, told, told
think, thought, thought
throw, threw, thrown
understand, understood, understood
wake, woke *or* waked, waked
wear, wore, worn
win, won, won
wind, wound, wound
write, wrote, written

appendix 3
Summary of Conjunctions

There are three groups of conjunctions, each with specific rules for punctuation.

Coordinating Conjunctions

There are exactly seven coordinating conjunctions:

> and
> but
> so (= that's why)
> for (= because)
> yet (= but)
> or
> nor*

Use:

1. Join two independent clauses with a comma and a coordinating conjunction.

   Examples: Her family owns a small factory, <u>and</u> she manages it.

                This might look easy, <u>but</u> it's actually rather difficult.

2. If there isn't an independent clause after the coordinating conjunction, don't use a comma before it.

   Examples: Her family owns a small factory <u>and</u> is thinking of expanding.

                This looks easy <u>but</u> is actually rather difficult.

3. In a series of three or more nouns, adjectives, verbs, or phrases, use commas to separate each item; this structure occurs with *and* or *or.*

   Examples: We'll go to Tunisia, Morocco, <u>or</u> Egypt.

                Their business imports fabric, produces clothing, <u>and</u> sells the clothing locally.

Nor is used somewhat differently.

1. with different subjects:

   a. Alice won't go to Ghana this year, <u>nor</u> will John.

   b. <u>Neither</u> Alice <u>nor</u> John will go to Ghana this year.

2. with different verbs:

   a. Alice didn't call, <u>nor</u> did she write.

   b. Alice <u>neither</u> called <u>nor</u> wrote.

3. with different objects:

   a. John can't send a fax, <u>nor</u> can he send an e-mail.

   b. John can send <u>neither</u> a fax <u>nor</u> an e-mail.

Subordinating Conjunctions

These are some of the many subordinating conjunctions.

because	when	by the time
although	whenever	as soon as (= immediately after)
as (= because)	before	until
since (= because)	after	as (= while; when)
even though	while (= when)	
while (= although)		if
whereas		unless (= if not)
		in case

Use:

1. If you begin a sentence with a subordinating conjunction, use a comma to separate the dependent and independent clauses.

   Example: <u>Because</u> she wanted to do business in Asia, she studied Asian languages and culture.

2. If the subordinating conjunction is in the middle of the sentence, there is usually no comma.

   Example: She studied Asian languages and culture <u>because</u> she wanted to do business in Asia.

Exception: There is often a comma before a subordinating conjunction of contrast.

Example: The New Kingdom was a period of military success and power in Egypt, <u>whereas</u> the Old Kingdom had been a time of defeat and failure.

Adverbial Conjunctions (Conjunctive Adverbs)

These are some of the many adverbial conjunctions.

in addition
moreover   } = and
furthermore
also

however
nevertheless* } = but
even so*
(*Use these in a surprising situation.)

therefore
consequently } = that's why
thus
as a result
for this reason

in contrast

on the other hand

in other words
that is
i.e.

for example
for instance
e.g.

first
next
afterwards
finally
then (no comma)

mostly
for the most part
to some extent (= partly)
to a large extent (= mostly)

in short
in conclusion

Use:

There are three main ways to use adverbial conjunctions: at the beginning of a sentence, at the beginning of an independent clause, or in the middle of an independent clause. Some conjunctions may appear at the end of a sentence.

Examples: The museum has an extensive collection of religious art. <u>In addition</u>, it houses a fine but small collection of genre paintings.

The exhibit of Egyptian art is extremely rare and valuable; <u>consequently</u>, security will be extraordinarily tight.

Everyone dreams every night. Many people, <u>however</u>, do not remember their dreams in the morning.

Everyone dreams every night. Many people do not remember their dreams in the morning, <u>however</u>.

photo credits